HISTORY OF THE WORLD

Civilizations of Asia

CHERRYTREE BOOKS

A Cherrytree Book

This edition adapted by
A S Publishing

First published by Editoriale Jaca Book s.p.a. Milan
© Editoriale Jaca 1987
First English edition published in United States
by Raintree Publishers
English translation © Raintree Publishers Limited Partnership
Translation by Hess-Inglin Translation Service

This edition first published 1990
by Cherrytree Press Ltd
a subsidiary of
The Chivers Company Ltd
Windsor Bridge Road
Bath, Avon BA2 3AX

Copyright © Cherrytree Press Ltd 1990

British Library Cataloguing in Publication Data
Civilization of Asia.
 1. Asian civilization, history
 I. Williams, Brian II. Series (History of the World) III. Grandi
 civilta dell'Asia. *English*
 950

ISBN 0-7451-5105-1

Printed in Hong Kong by Imago Publishing Ltd

CONTENTS

Years B.C. and A.D.	INDIA	CHINA	JAPAN
	PALEOLITHIC 300,000 The most ancient finds	**PALEOLITHIC** 1,800,000 The most ancient finds	**PALEOLITHIC** 400,000 The most ancient finds 7000 **EARLY JOMON PERIOD**
6000		6000 **NEOLITHIC** First agricultural practices First ceramics	
3500	3500 **NEOLITHIC** From the Iranian plateau, Stone Age culture spreads into India		
3000			
2500			
2300	2300 **CIVILIZATION OF THE INDUS VALLEY**		
2000			
1700	1700-1500 **ARYAN INVASION**		
1500		1500 **SHANG DYNASTY** Bronze artifacts and first towns Writing	1500 **MIDDLE JOMON PERIOD** Elements of transition towards the Neolithic period
1100		1100 **REIGN OF THE ZHOU**	
1000	1000 **VEDIC CIVILIZATION** First villages and societies Hinduism	770 **SPRING AND AUTUMN PERIOD** Religion	1000 **NEOLITHIC-LATE JOMON** Rice growing begins
700			
	560-486 **BUDDHA and Buddhism**		
500	540-486 Mahavira and Jainism	485 **THE WARRING STATES PERIOD** Confucius, Taoism, and the classic age of Chinese philosophy	
400			
350			
	321 **THE MAURYA EMPIRE** Founded by Chandragupta		
300	269 Asoka spreads Buddhism		300 **YAYOI EPOCH** Agriculture develops and bronze comes into use
250		221 **QIN, THE FIRST EMPIRE**	
200		206 **THE HAN DYNASTY** Confucianism The spread of Buddhism Trade with the Mediterranean Early classic age in China	
100			
50	50 **THE SATAVAHANA EMPIRE** (Southern India)		Shinto religion
0			
50	50 **THE KUSHAN EMPIRE** (Northern India) Greek-Indian art The birth of Hinduism		
100			
200		220-265 **THE THREE KINGDOMS** Political division The importance of the south increases nomadic kingdoms to the north Increase in Asian trade Revival of Taoism The spread of Buddhism	
300	320 **THE GUPTA EMPIRE** "Golden age" of India		300 **AGE OF THE ANCIENT TOMBS** Widespread use of iron Wealth and power Transformation of society
400	467 The Gupta Empire falls under pressure from the nomads of the steppes		538-552 Spread of Buddhism
500			574-622 **THE SHOTOKU REGENCY** Modernizing the country The Seventeen Article Constitution Relationship with China
600			

INDOCHINA

PALEOLITHIC
400,000 The most ancient finds

3000   **NEOLITHIC**
Arrival of populations from China
Rice growing begins

1000   **THE DONG SON
CIVILIZATION**
The spread of bronze

Contacts with Indonesia and the
Pacific islands begin

300   **INFLUENCE OF INDIA AND
CHINA**
Writing, kingdoms, Hinduism and
Buddhism, art

centre and west	east
	250 EARLY VIETNAMESE KINGDOM
	111 Annexation by China and political-cultural dependence on China for almost 1000 years
Indian merchants control trade	
250 THE FUNAN EMPIRE Based on commercial and maritime relationships	
600 THE KINGDOM OF TCHENLA Early Cambodian Khmer reign	

INDONESIA

PALEOLITHIC
1,800,000 The most ancient finds

2500   **NEOLITHIC**
Arrival of farming populations
from Indochina

500   The spread of bronze from
Indochina

250   Influence of the Funan Empire in
the North

AUSTRALIA AND OCEANIA

PALEOLITHIC
30,000 The earliest evidence of
settlement in Australia

2000   The settlement of Micronesia and
of part of Melanesia

1000   The settlement of all of Melanesia

300   Populating the Marquesas Islands

400   Populating the Hawaiian Islands

800-850   The last islands to be populated

ASIA
FROM THE PALEOLITHIC
PERIOD TO A.D. 600

In blue: late Paleolithic period
In purple-blue: Neolithic period
The coloured stripes indicate the influence
of the corresponding civilizations.

Years B.C. and A.D.
6000
3500
3000
2500
2300
2000
1700
1500
1100
1000
700
500
400
350
300
250
200
100
50
0
100
200
300
400
500
600

5

ASIA

The Regions of Asia

Asia is the world's largest continent, a vast landmass with many islands. It extends from Africa and Europe in the west to the Pacific Ocean in the east and has a variety of climates and landscapes. Mountain chains cross the continent east to west, dividing it into several large regions. These include India, China, Indochina, and the steppes of Central Asia. Islands include Japan and Indonesia.

Isolated from the ocean, Central Asia has limited rainfall. The northern part is covered by steppes and has enough plant life to feed wandering livestock. The drier southern part is covered by deserts and mountain chains.

India, located south of the Himalayas, is almost a continent in itself. North to south, it stretches for nearly 3,200 kilometres. Its climate ranges from alpine around the Himalayas to tropical at the coast.

China occupies much of eastern Asia. Seasonal temperatures differ greatly. Winters in China are much colder than anywhere in India. Rainfall is also varied. In the north, farmland is arid. To the south, in the Yangtze River basin and the surrounding mountains, water is abundant.

Indochina is crossed by forest-covered mountain chains running parallel to the coast. Human settlements occur mainly on wide inland plateaus, coastal plains, and river deltas. To the east stretch a series of islands.

The Monsoons

The seasonal winds, or monsoons, are the main influence on the climate of India and all the far eastern Asian regions, from the equator to the temperate areas of the north. From October to May, it rains very little in India. The land becomes dry, the temperature rises, and a hot wind blows from land to sea. In June, the winds bring in moisture from the Indian Ocean. Rains begin and the wet season lasts longer than two months. The temperature drops, and plant life is revived. The monsoons carry humid ocean air northwards in the summer, bringing the rains.

Australia

South of Indonesia is Australia. This island is a relatively young land. Humans settled there only recently.

forest in the temperate regions

equatorial forest

desert

CENTRA

INDIA

grassland

INDIAN OCEAN

monsoon line

farmland in a mountain region

farmland in a flood plain

JAPAN

monsoon line

PACIFIC OCEAN

monsoon line

ASIA

CHINA

volcano

PHILIPPINES

INDOCHINA

steppe of central Asia

INDONESIA

Indian savanna

monsoon line

AUSTRALIA

farmland

grassland

desert

woods, equatorial forest, savannas

barren high mountain areas

steppe

volcanoes and volcanic areas

monsoon zone enclosed
within the shaded lines

high mountains

THE PALEOLITHIC PERIOD

Asia, Ancient Land of Human Prehistory

Asia was once thought by some to be the cradle of humanity. In 1891 in Java, Eugène Dubois, a Dutch army surgeon, discovered the remains of a prehistoric human being. Experts considered this creature, called Java man, to be one of the links between humans and apes. Years later, however, similar remains over two million years old were found in Africa. From research done in Africa, the stages of human evolution can now be identified. First came *Homo habilis*, a savanna hunter and tool-user who lived in groups and built simple dwellings. Then came *Homo erectus*, who discovered fire, made better stone tools, and whose brain presumably formed more complicated thoughts. Finally, *Homo sapiens* or modern humans, developed.

Homo Erectus in Java and China

So far, no fossil remains of *Homo habilis* have been found in Asia. The most ancient fossil find in Java is 1,800,000 years old. It is called Meganthropus, but experts are not sure whether it is an ancestor of *Homo erectus* or if it belongs to an earlier group of creatures known as Australopithecines. The most ancient groups of *Homo erectus* were present in Java about 1,100,000 years ago.

Northern China is another important source of *Homo erectus* remains and has even provided evidence of the stone tools that were used. Two teeth found in Yunnan province date back 1,700,000 years. Lantian man, discovered in Shaanxi, appeared about 700,000 years ago. The famous Peking man, or Sinanthropus, found in 1921 in Zhoukoudian, lived more recently than the others. This group lived between 500,000 and 200,000 years ago and the remains of over forty individuals have been studied.

Homo Sapiens in China

As *Homo sapiens* evolved, groups of these people spread all over China. They were expert tool-makers. All over northern China, finely crafted blades, called microliths, were made. They were mounted on bone or wooden handles and were precise, useful tools. Evidence of fire-making and seasonal camps have been discovered.

The Paleolithic Period in India and Japan

No fossil remains prior to the Mesolithic period have been found in India. What scientists know about the country's ancient human settlements comes from the many stone tools found there. The oldest of these tools, found in the Soan River area, are large, slightly sharpened pebbles from 200,000 to 300,000 years ago. Later, especially in the southern regions, more advanced tools, called bifacial tools, were sharpened on both sides.

The oldest Japanese stone tools, which are about 400,000 years old, are pebbles with sharp, rough-cut edges. Pebbles of this kind include hand-axes made between 50,000 and 35,000 B.C.

This map shows the changing land and sea levels in southeast Asia and Australia.

Populating Southeast Asia and Australia

The remains of *Homo erectus* in Indochina are more than 400,000 years old. Between 30,000 and 10,000 B.C., *Homo sapiens* appeared in the Philippines, Borneo, and Java. Here, by 20,000 B.C., the so-called Wadjak man had features similar to those of the aboriginal Australians living today. Within about 30,000 years of the end of the Paleolithic period, the first humans had settled in Australia.

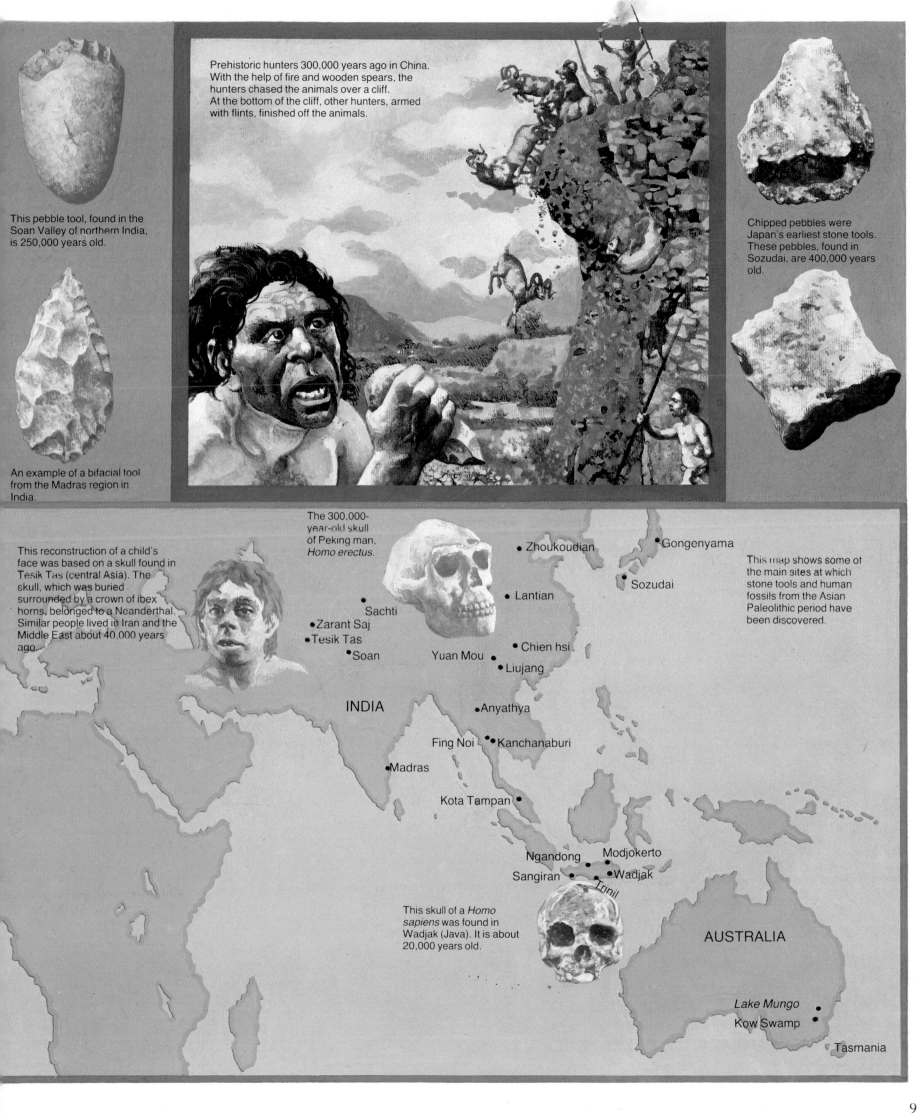

This pebble tool, found in the Soan Valley of northern India, is 250,000 years old.

An example of a bifacial tool from the Madras region in India.

Prehistoric hunters 300,000 years ago in China. With the help of fire and wooden spears, the hunters chased the animals over a cliff. At the bottom of the cliff, other hunters, armed with flints, finished off the animals.

Chipped pebbles were Japan's earliest stone tools. These pebbles, found in Sozudai, are 400,000 years old.

This reconstruction of a child's face was based on a skull found in Tesik Tas (central Asia). The skull, which was buried surrounded by a crown of ibex horns, belonged to a Neanderthal. Similar people lived in Iran and the Middle East about 40,000 years ago.

The 300,000-year-old skull of Peking man, *Homo erectus*.

This map shows some of the main sites at which stone tools and human fossils from the Asian Paleolithic period have been discovered.

Zhoukoudian

Gongenyama

Sozudai

Lantian

Sachti

Zarant Saj

Tesik Tas

Soan

Yuan Mou

Chien hsi

Liujang

INDIA

Anyathya

Fing Noi

Kanchanaburi

Madras

Kota Tampan

Ngandong

Modjokerto

Sangiran

Wadjak

Trinil

This skull of a *Homo sapiens* was found in Wadjak (Java). It is about 20,000 years old.

AUSTRALIA

Lake Mungo

Kow Swamp

Tasmania

Around 20,000 B.C., during the last ice age, Japan was still connected to the Asian mainland. The glaciers are shown in green.

SIBERIA   Hokkaido

KOREA   Honshu

Shikoku
Kyushu

PACIFIC OCEAN

By 10,000 B.C., Japan had completely separated from the mainland but still had a close relationship with it. Influences from the continent came through the ancient land routes. To the north, Japan was influenced by Siberia; to the south, by China and Korea.

The giant deer and the mammoth were typical animals in prehistoric Japan. During the glaciations, they migrated to Japan. The deer came from Korea; the mammoth came from northern Asia.

| 400,000 B.C. | PALEOLITHIC from the roughly cut pebbles of Sozudai to the finely cut tools of Iwajuku | 13,000 | MESOLITHIC great abundance of microliths |

In this illustration, a hunter skins an elk in southern Japan about 20,000 years ago. In the background, smoke rises from an active volcano.

The legend bar (*above*) shows the major periods of prehistory in Japan.

JAPAN FROM THE PALEOLITHIC PERIOD TO THE MIDDLE JOMON PERIOD

The Isolation of Japan

Japan, as it is known today, is an archipelago formed by four major islands and numerous smaller islands. This geographical arrangement emerged very recently.

In ancient times, Japan was part of the Eurasian continent. From the Kamchatka Peninsula to Indonesia, the land facing the Pacific Ocean stretched in a continuous line. But little by little, the gradual rise of the wide China plain caused rift valleys to appear. These rifts filled with ocean water. In this way, the Okhotsk Sea, the Japan Sea, and the China Sea were formed, separating the coast from the interior. Japan was already displaying a "sickle" shape 500,000 years ago, and by then was connected to the continent only by its northern and southern tips. In the meantime, the land kept changing: the Pacific rifts grew deeper, small pieces of land separated from the

continent, and the land that was to become Japan, shaken by violent volcanic activity, broke into many islands. Japan probably became totally isolated from mainland Asia around 15,000 years ago.

Paleolithic Japan

It was once thought that people inhabited Japan only recently. But fossils and other remains found in the past few decades are evidence of much earlier human settlements. Today, sites dating back to the Paleolithic period are known throughout Japan.

Fossil remains of Japan's early inhabitants show some Neanderthal features. These Paleolithic people spread throughout Japan while the land was still changing. They most certainly lived in danger of volcanoes. In the Gumma region, stone tools were found in ash layers and hardened lava flows from volcanic eruptions.

Three vases of the middle Jomon (1500-1000 B.C.) with cord-marked decoration typical of this period.

7000 PROTO JOMON	5000 EARLY JOMON	1500 MIDDLE JOMON	1000 RECENT AND LATE JOMON	500 B.C.

By the seashore, men and women of the early Jomon period gather shellfish. In the foreground is a heap of empty shells. Huge piles of these discarded shells have been found throughout Japan. To the right can be seen the thatched dwellings of the village, erected above shallow pits.

This clay mask and figurine date back to the late Jomon period (1000-500 B.C.). Both objects were used in religious rituals.

Evolution of the Mesolithic Period

During this period, hunting was still the main means of survival, but tools changed greatly. From the simple pebbles of the late Paleolithic period developed the finely crafted tools of the Mesolithic period, which started around 13,000 B.C. These changes, along with the appearance of new objects, suggest that trading routes—either by land or by river— also began at this time.

The Early and Middle Jomon Period

As people's skills and the trade routes developed, a new way of life began in Japan. This new period was known for its simple pottery and the method of decorating it, using cords to mark the clay. In fact, this method gave the Jomon period its name. In Japanese, *Jomon* means "rope decoration".

As the Jomon period began (around 7000 B.C.), the human population continued to expand. People began to settle for long periods in places where their needs could be met. A typical settlement was found at the foot of a hill, close to a river, or on the seashore. There, the mountains offered caves or other shelters. The forest-covered slopes were well-stocked with game. The river and the sea supplied fish and shellfish, a main part of the human diet.

In spite of its cold winters and hot summers, Japan's natural resources made life easy. Because of this, it was many years before people learned to depend on farming for their food. Until the middle Jomon period (around 1000 B.C.), the people were too well fed with fish to worry about starting a farming economy. Nevertheless, villages started to appear.

From around 1600 B.C., rice was grown in the moist areas of the Yangtze River basin.

A Neolithic village in northern China surrounded by a ditch for protection from wild animals.

A bone ploughshare belonging to the Hemudu culture dates back to 5000 B.C.

These two ritual objects of jade were found in the Yangtze River basin. On the left is a Zong, the use of which is still unknown. Below is an axe dating from 2500-2000 B.C.

THE NEOLITHIC PERIOD IN CHINA

The Beginnings of Agriculture and Ceramics

Remains of the early Neolithic societies in China are clearly visible in the Huang He (Yellow River) basin. There, human communities became closely tied to the land. At first this tie was temporary, but later people abandoned the nomadic life completely. The most ancient cultures in the Huang He basin date back to 6000 B.C.

Typical artifacts of these first communities are simple clay objects decorated with impressions of cord, wicker, or combs. These ceramics are very different from the beautiful vases of the Yangshao culture that eventually developed in Henan province.

At this time, villages started appearing. In northern China, they were numerous and close together. In fact, excavations show that they were often not more than 9 kilometres apart.

Some were large, such as Banpo, which covered 3 hectares, or Lintong, which covered 5 hectares. Some were surrounded by moats or ditches as protection against wild animals or human attackers.

Little by little, the shape of the houses changed from circular to square, and they were eventually built more above ground. Wooden columns or poles supported a thatched roof, and a central hole served as a chimney. As the roofs rose above ground level, the walls were built of a mixture of clay, stones, and reeds placed between wooden poles. Many villages also had a community house. This large, square building was often found at the village's centre.

Growth of China's Culture

China's climate, which was warmer than it is today, favoured the development of agricul-

12

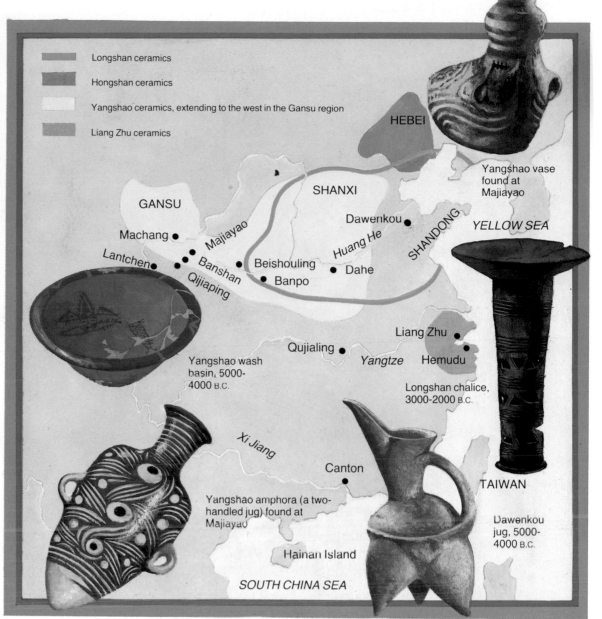

This map shows the most important centres of the Chinese Neolithic period and the areas where different types of ceramics developed and overlapped.

Map legend:
- Longshan ceramics
- Hongshan ceramics
- Yangshao ceramics, extending to the west in the Gansu region
- Liang Zhu ceramics

Map labels: HEBEI, SHANXI, GANSU, SHANDONG, YELLOW SEA, Machang, Majiayao, Dawenkou, Lantchen, Banshan, Beishouling, Dahe, Huang He, Qijiaping, Banpo, Liang Zhu, Qujialing, Hemudu, Yangtze, Xi Jiang, Canton, TAIWAN, Hainan Island, SOUTH CHINA SEA

Yangshao vase found at Majiayao

Longshan chalice, 3000-2000 B.C.

Yangshao wash basin, 5000-4000 B.C.

Yangshao amphora (a two-handled jug) found at Majiayao

Dawenkou jug, 5000-4000 B.C.

A carved jade bracelet

These stone axes, from the middle of the third millennium B.C., were found near Hong Kong in southern China.

This painted ceramic vase was found in the Gansu Province along the course of the Wei River. The decoration is believed to be the most ancient Chinese image of a dragon.

ture. In the middle and lower basin of the Yangtze, rice was grown as early as 5000 B.C. About the same time, around the Huang He River, millet was cultivated. The gathering of vegetables, hunting, and fishing completed the diet. A settled life-style and free time in slack farming months helped people develop such crafts as weaving, ceramics, and dyeing.

The Chinese civilization was moving forward at a great rate. At the same time, people showed an increasing interest in the past, especially in respect for their ancestors and the dead. Children who died in their youth or who were sacrificed in rituals during construction of a home were buried in jars inside the house or near by. Older children and adults were buried in special sites, in tombs, or in large jars. Neolithic cemeteries also show that women played an important role in Chinese society. Often burials of women outnumbered those of men. Through the centuries, however, the number of male burials grew as more importance was given to men in social life.

Changes Around the End of the Neolithic Period

By 2700 B.C., people were skilled in using the potter's wheel. With it, they produced a new kind of ceramic that was thin, shiny, and often only one colour. The most beautiful examples of this period come from the sites of Dawenkou and Longshan in Shandong province (northeast China). Also at this time, people domesticated horses and sheep.

It is difficult to trace the progress of the human populations that lived outside the central areas. It is certain, though, that the groups in the various regions were very active, from the Yangshao culture on the upper Huang He to the complex Yangtze cultures (at Daxi and Qujialing) and those of the Canton (Guangzhou) region. For example, improved kilns and the expert management of fire quickly spread the use of bronze around 1500 B.C. Such activities speeded the progress of Chinese culture.

This decorated vase and clay figurine of a mother-goddess was found in Nindowari, which was possibly a pilgrimage site.

An early village scene in northwest India. The introduction of agriculture changed everyday life.

THE NEOLITHIC PERIOD IN INDIA AND SOUTHEAST ASIA

A Major Change in India

After the Ice Age, important changes took place all over southern Asia. Around the end of the Paleolithic period and the beginning of the Mesolithic period, people in India specialized in various kinds of fishing and hunting of both large and small animals. Wild plants became an important food source, and grains were gathered to be ground or chopped. The people also made tools to cut stones, wood, bones, and skins. The most important of these tools was the microlith, a small, finely cut stone blade made of quartz or flint.

The signs of a major change were apparent. In Rajasthan, domesticated sheep and goats became an important part of the economy. New cooking methods were invented, and from time to time, the first rudimentary forms of hand-worked pottery appeared. By this time, people lived in huts with walls made of bamboo and covered with mud. They began to settle permanently and made the first attempts at farming. Trees were felled and burned, and the land was farmed for short periods, with the growing of rice beginning in the Ganges valley.

The Birth of Agriculture

This way of life was to continue for a long time in India, especially in the more remote central and southern regions. To the west of the Iranian plateau, however, agriculture gradually advanced. The earliest traces of farming and stable settlements east of Iran have been found in Afghanistan and Pakistan and date back to 3500-3000 B.C. These farming populations were probably small scattered groups, who brought new methods from Iran. At first, they established nomadic camps, but little by little, villages grew. Houses were first made of clay and later of bricks, and the size of villages slowly increased. Potters' wheels were used to manufacture pots and other vessels, and the first copper tools appeared. These people also kept some animals such as goats, pigs, and cows.

Villages spread throughout the Iranian plateau and into Baluchistan. To the north, the settlement of farmers was stopped by the mountains, but they were able to settle in the Punjab region. From there, they moved towards the plains, developing irrigation techniques to control water supplies for crops.

None of the human settlements were larger than villages, with the exception of Mundigak, in what is today Afghanistan. Within a few centuries, this network of settlements would grow to become the valley's first city complex.

On an inland Indochina plateau, colonists from the north clear forest by slashing and burning.

1) Shoulder axe from Samrong Sen; 2) stone tool from Luang Prabang; 3) jade bifacial from Yunnan; 4) scraper from Som Jo, near Hoa Binh; 5) arrowhead from Trieng-Xen, near Hoa Binh; 6 and 7) Neolithic clay bowls from Ban Chieng; 8) Neolithic vase from Ban Chieng.

The Mesolithic Period in Southeast Asia

After the glaciations, the Indochina peninsula became more accessible. Between 5000 and 3000 B.C., people spread throughout this region, bringing with them new ideas and techniques. Their tools were more finely crafted, and the materials used to make them were chosen with more care. These people, who probably came from southern China, later spread towards the Pacific islands. The site of Hoa Binh (modern Vietnam) is especially rich in finds from this group. About the same time, another migrating group of people moved southwards. They were using short axes with smoothed blades and other tools made of mother of pearl or bone. They already had a primitive form of pottery. These people were named after the Bacson region, where numerous burial caves were uncovered. They left traces throughout Indochina.

The Spread of Agriculture

With the coming of agriculture, people in different regions now shared similar ways of life. For example, rice cultivation started at roughly the same time in Indochina as in China and India, perhaps even before. Better farming methods also called for better tools. Axes, which were at first egg-shaped, were now shaped more like diamonds. Many of these axes also had extensions, which made it easier to tie them to handles. With improved tools, woodworking and ceramics were perfected between 2500 and 1000 B.C.

From the mountain regions, people moved towards the lowlands and the open plains, becoming more skilled in farming. They still grew rice on dry land but also learned to control irrigation. This allowed rice to be grown on flooded fields. From the Malaya Peninsula, farming populations moved into Indonesia.

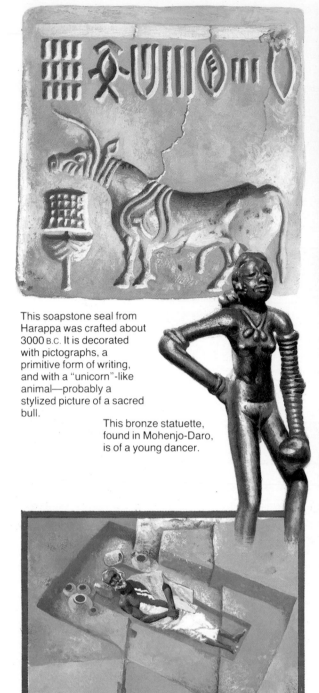

This soapstone seal from Harappa was crafted about 3000 B.C. It is decorated with pictographs, a primitive form of writing, and with a "unicorn"-like animal—probably a stylized picture of a sacred bull.

This bronze statuette, found in Mohenjo-Daro, is of a young dancer.

This soapstone bust depicts the "king-priest" of Mohenjo-Daro.

Indus River

Ravi River

Harappa

Sutlej River

The city of Mohenjo-Daro was built on various levels. *Below:* A street in the lower city, showing the canal system, which supplied water to almost every house.

Mohenjo-Daro

Cianu-Daro

ARABIAN SEA

Lothal

Areas where the civilization of the Indus Valley spread are shown in green.

Left: The peoples of the Indus Valley did not burn their dead on pyres. They buried them underground. This drawing reconstructs a burial chamber found in Harappa.

THE CIVILIZATION OF THE INDUS VALLEY

Urban Civilization

Around 2500 B.C., an urban civilization developed in the area between Pakistan and the Indian states of Punjab and Gujarat. Earlier, this same area had seen farming practices develop and the first villages appear. This urban civilization had complex forms of art and religion, and its cities were equipped with sewers, granaries, and sanitary facilities.

The existence of such an advanced civilization in India, which had not yet suffered the disturbance of Indo-European invasions, was unknown until the early 20th century. Eventually, through excavations led by the British archaeologist Sir John Marshall, this civiliza-tion's remains were uncovered. Though a great amount of material was found in these excavations, not much is yet known about the civilization. For example, the writing of the Indus Valley civilization (so called because its towns were erected along the course of the Indus River) has not yet been deciphered. Experts have tried to break the code working with pictographs found on seals and graffiti. But so far, no final results have been obtained.

As for the ethnic nature of the Indus Valley people, it is likely that they belonged to the Dravida family. This group of humans appeared in India during ancient times. The people had dark complexions and long, straight hair. They were of medium height and spoke a variety of "Dravidan" languages or dialects.

The main centres of Indus civilization were the cities of Harappa and Mohenjo-Daro. Although over 500 kilometres apart, the two cities show many similarities in their cultures. These similarities sprang from an easy com-munication along the river routes and a common government under the same political and religious authority. The urban and social structure of Harappa and Mohenjo-Daro was based on an economy of trading and agricul-ture. The main crops were wheat and barley, as shown by granaries which were found

The granaries of Harappa were built on platforms raised above the ground. They were divided into blocks by streets.

This drawing shows the ground floor of a typical house in Mohenjo-Daro. Note the vestibule and the room for the housekeeper. The central courtyard was paved with bricks. Around the courtyard were the small servants' rooms and the kitchen. The master's quarters were on the first floor.

Above: An artist's reconstruction of the city of Mohenjo-Daro at the height of its splendour, around 2000 B.C. A fortress stands in the foreground. The houses here are rather large. In the lower part of the city, poorer people lived in crowded quarters. Their houses had only two rooms. *Top left:* This soapstone seal, from Mohenjo-Daro, dates from the third millennium B.C.

during excavations in Mohenjo-Daro. As for the military structure, the Indus Valley civilization seems to have been completely peaceful. The few weapons found seem more likely to have been used for hunting than for war.

Art and Religion

Experts working on the Indus Valley excavations have noted many similarities between its culture and that of more recent times. Art found in the Indus Valley, for example, closely resembles Indian art of the last 1,500 years. In addition, religious figurines found in Harappa and Mohenjo-Daro are very like those of later Hinduism. Evidence of

cults surrounding a Great Goddess, trees, water, and a male divinity further suggest a connection between this early religion and Hinduism, which has similar cults in its teachings. The fact that Hinduism as a religion did not emerge until hundreds of years after the end of the Indus civilization is a question puzzling many archaeologists.

The End of the Indus Valley Civilization

The Indus Valley civilization, so highly developed and "modern", disappeared suddenly around 1500 B.C. It appears that after a short period of decline, it quickly collapsed

and vanished. Scholars have several theories to explain such an event. One possible cause was the arrival of warlike Indo-European or Aryan tribes. These tribes violently colonized northwestern India. Some scholars suggest that the Aryan invaders coming from the plains of the Ganges may have destroyed vital water sources. Still other sources suggest that some sort of ecological disaster due to deforestation caused the civilization's collapse. Perhaps the answer is a combination of all these factors.

HIMALAYAS

Indus River

Ganges River

ARABIAN SEA

Narmada River

A thriving Indo-European village near a riverbank. The houses are made of clay with thatched roofs. In the foreground, father and son return home in a cart pulled by oxen. Beyond them, a man is ploughing with oxen by the river, and some women are doing laundry. On the threshing-floor in front of the houses, rice is winnowed and then stored under a shelter. Boats sailing on the river provide one of the main means of transport for people and goods. Originally nomadic shepherds, the Indo-European tribes eventually settled in India. Here they learned to combine livestock-rearing and agriculture, abandoning nomadism. The villages which developed at that time (1500-1000 B.C.) are still a typical feature of Indian life today.

Map: Around 1500 B.C., numerous groups of Indo-European nomadic tribes arrived from the west. They spread through and conquered the territories of the Indus Valley civilization. Some of them reached as far as the plains of the Ganges.

INDIA: THE INDO-EUROPEAN INVADERS

The Arrival of the Indo-Europeans

Around 1500 B.C., the Indus Valley civilization disappeared. About this same time, India was invaded by several waves of nomadic and rather warlike people coming from the west. In general, the invaders' movement was from west to east, with small digressions to the south. The military superiority of these peoples was based mainly on the use of horse-drawn war chariots.

Within a rather short time (1500 to 1000 B.C.), the Indo-European tribes occupied the whole Indus River region, most of the plains through which the Ganges River flows (north-central India), and some neighbouring regions. The newcomers, called Aryans, were nomadic tribes living as herders and hunters. Their simple, unrefined culture thus took the place of the highly developed culture of the Indus Valley. But once they reached India, they settled and built stable villages.

On the Indian continent, more particularly in its north-central regions, these tribes lived in villages with a square layout. Often these villages were well fortified, with four main gateways. Houses were built of wood, bamboo, or clay. These materials were also used for other buildings used for cult worship and meetings. Because of the perishable nature of

The Indo-European tribes that settled in India were divided into three main social groups, commonly called castes. The Brahmans were the priests, who maintained relationships with the world of the gods for the whole community. Among them were the rishi, or seers, and the ascetics. (Ascetics were holy men, who practised rigid self-denial as a religious act.) The Kshatriya had the military power. This caste consisted of warriors, groups of which were led by a raja, or ruler. The Vaisya had the economic power because they farmed the land, raised the cattle, and carried on businesses. Each caste had its own colour category: the Brahmans wore white, the Kshatriya wore red, and the Vaisya wore yellow.

their construction materials, no trace of the dwellings remains today.

Vedic Society

The social organization of the Indo-European tribes is usually called Vedic. The name comes from the people's sacred texts, the Vedas, and the social order was wholly based on their teachings. The name *Veda* comes from the Sanskrit word *vid*, which means "to know". The Vedas are a collection of supposedly divinely revealed truths, gathered and ordered by seers called *rishi*. The text of the Vedas is practically the only cultural treasure of this period (1500-1000 B.C.) that remains.

As the Indo-European tribes settled on the Indian continent, they created a culture based on the rural village. Within the village, the family was the main structure around which all everyday activities revolved. Work in the fields was often done cooperatively, and the economy was almost completely based on farming. Religion had a major role in Vedic society, and the priests held important social positions. The Vedic religion was Hinduism.

Division into Castes

A typical feature of Vedic society was the caste system. By this system, society was divided into three major groups, each with various rights and duties. The Sanskrit word for what in English is called caste is *jati*, which means "birth" or "origin", stressing the fact that a person's caste is determined by birth.

During the early period of Vedic society, castes were not yet fixed. Instead, the classes were based on the three basic social activities: religion (priests), attack and defence (war-riors), and sustaining the population (farmers, herders, artisans). But as time passed, this class system became more rigid and hardened into a caste system around 1000 B.C. In this system, birth determines a person's caste once and forever, and it cannot be changed. Marriages are permitted only within the same caste, and the offspring automatically belong to their parents' caste. The three principal castes are: the priests (Brahmans), who maintain relationships with the world of gods and goddesses; the warriors and rulers (Kshatriya) who attend to war and government; and the merchants and farmers (Vaisya). At the bottom were labourers (Sudra).

ATHARVA VEDA

Upanishad

Aranyaka

Brahmana

YAJUR VEDA

Upanishad

Aranyaka

Brahmana

RIG VEDA

Upanishad

Aranyaka

Brahmana

SAMA VEDA

Upanishad

Aranyaka

Brahmana

Top: The Indo-European religion in India was based on four sacred books called the Vedas. The word *veda* is a Sanskrit word meaning "knowledge". In the picture (*above*), the Vedas are shown like a large tree. The branches represent the subgroups which comprise the four Vedas and the subdivision within each Veda. The Veda text is written on rectangular sheets. Some were ornate with decoration, and some of the wealthiest Brahmans owned sheets with writing in gold letters. *Above:* A young Brahman sits in the typical position for concentration and meditation.

INDIA: HINDUISM

The Four Vedas

The first three books of the Veda—Rig Veda, Sama Veda, and Yajur Veda—preserve the religious, philosophical, and literary history of the Indo-European people. The fourth Veda, the Atharva Veda, was added later. Even today, however, some Brahmans do not consider this Veda sacred.

The Vedas, and particularly the Rig Veda, are considered Hinduism's most sacred books. The teachings contained in the Vedas, however, are not like those of the Bible. In that book, God practically dictates to the prophets the message for the chosen people. Nor are they like the epics of Greek mythology, where the narrators were poets. The *rishi* (or seer) is neither prophet nor poet. He does not need a chosen people nor a listening crowd. His is a personal experience, which occurs under certain mental and physical conditions. This experience is called *sruti*, or the revelation of

knowledge. According to myth, this occurred four times—corresponding to the four great periods into which the Vedic Indians divide life in the world. These are: the golden age (kritayuga), in which the Rig Veda was revealed; the silver age (tretayuga), in which the Yajur Veda was revealed; the bronze age (dvaparayuga), in which the Atharva Veda was revealed; and the iron age (kaliyuga) in which the Sama Veda was revealed. It can be said that each Veda reveals a particular aspect of religious life.

Hindu Deities

Hinduism is *polytheistic*, which means it has many gods. Most gods, or deities, are males with the exception of Aditi, the mother of the gods. The great gods of the Rig Veda are Indra, Varuna, Agni, Surya, and Yama. Indra is the master of the gods, the supreme god of the heavens. He is the symbol of warriors and

Sacrificial offerings to the gods were very important in early Hinduism. Usually, the Brahmans would offer the main sacrifices, but some of them were offered by the ruler. The most well-known and spectacular sacrifice was the "sacrifice of the horse". In this ritual, the ruler, assisted by court Brahmans and warriors, would bless a horse, and then set it free to roam the kingdom. After a year, the animal was captured, richly adorned, and harnessed to a chariot. The horse then pulled the chariot, with the king riding in it, in a procession. At the end of the ceremony, the horse was sacrificed.

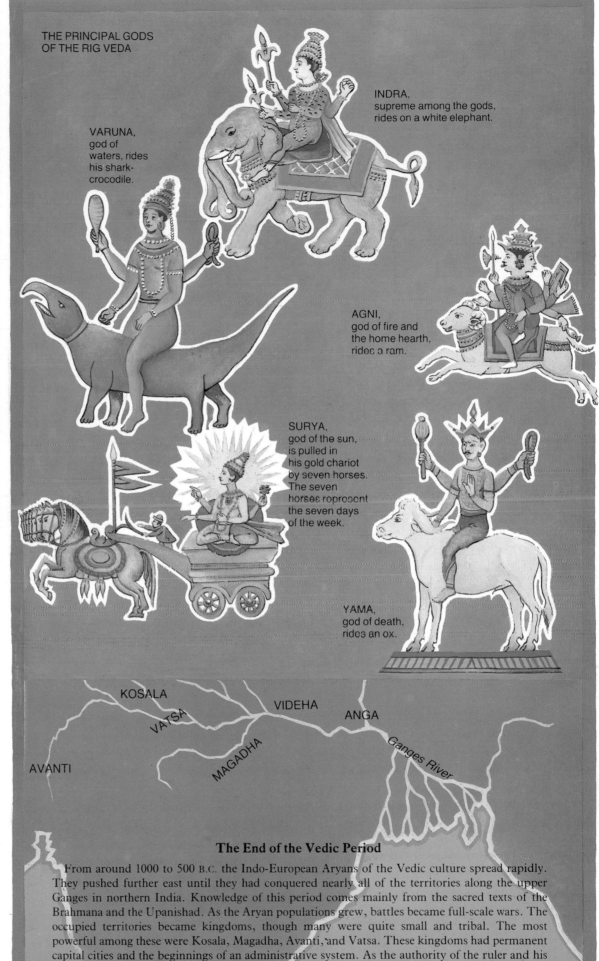

THE PRINCIPAL GODS OF THE RIG VEDA

INDRA, supreme among the gods, rides on a white elephant.

VARUNA, god of waters, rides his shark-crocodile.

AGNI, god of fire and the home hearth, rides a ram.

SURYA, god of the sun, is pulled in his gold chariot by seven horses. The seven horses represent the seven days of the week.

YAMA, god of death, rides an ox.

of heroes. He protects the Aryan peoples from their enemies and keeps order in the world by killing demons. Like the Roman god Jupiter, Indra is the master of lightning and uses it as a weapon to battle his enemies. Varuna is the supreme god of waters. He is the keeper of the Supreme Law, or dharma, which he himself established in the beginning. He has unlimited visual powers; the sun is his eye, and he knows the destiny of every person. Agni is the god of fire. He was an extremely powerful deity in the ancient world, where fire was an important element of life Surya is the god of the sun. His cult was among the most important for people of ancient times. Surya is the great eye in the sky which sees everything and surveys gods and mortals. Yama, the god of death, is connected to the mystery of death and all the symbols around it. He is also the father of the human race. The Rig Veda gods became less important in later Hinduism.

The End of the Vedic Period

From around 1000 to 500 B.C. the Indo-European Aryans of the Vedic culture spread rapidly. They pushed further east until they had conquered nearly all of the territories along the upper Ganges in northern India. Knowledge of this period comes mainly from the sacred texts of the Brahmana and the Upanishad. As the Aryan populations grew, battles became full-scale wars. The occupied territories became kingdoms, though many were quite small and tribal. The most powerful among these were Kosala, Magadha, Avanti, and Vatsa. These kingdoms had permanent capital cities and the beginnings of an administrative system. As the authority of the ruler and his court grew, the power of the tribal assemblies lessened.

Villages were still the most common settlements, but cities were also beginning to develop. In addition to using gold and copper, the Aryans of the late Vedic period knew how to work with tin, lead, silver, and especially iron. The farming of cereal crops flourished. Occupations became more specialized.

KOSALA
VATSA
VIDEHA
ANGA
MAGADHA
AVANTI
Ganges River

BUDDHISM AND JAINISM IN INDIA

The Life of Buddha

Around 500 B.C., northwestern India experienced a deep religious crisis. The Vedic world had lost most of its energy. Religion was often reduced to a formal routine which the Brahman caste carried out without any enthusiasm.

Reaction to this crisis in Indian society witnessed the birth of several preachings intended to renew the spirit of religion. The most important of these new religious trends was Buddhism. Its founder was Gautama Siddhartha, the king of a small realm in northern India.

Gautama Siddhartha was born around 560 B.C. in Kapilavastu and was raised with all the honours due to a young prince. His family, fearing that contact with the world would disturb him, kept the boy aloof from all of life's difficulties. He passed the first twenty-nine years of his life within his father's royal palace, ignorant of what was happening in the outside world. He married Jasodhara, a girl of noble birth. Soon they had a son.

One day, curiosity drew the prince beyond the walls of the royal palace. In the city streets, Gautama suddenly faced the daily reality of human life. He met a sick man and learned that the body could get sick. Next he met an old man and had to face the pains of old age.

To the left: **(1)** Prince Gautama Siddhartha, the Buddha, lived and taught in India in the fifth century B.C. **(2)** Before he was born, Gautama's mother dreamed he entered her womb in the form of a white elephant. **(3)** The young prince sits in the garden of the royal palace of his father. **(4)** The prince meets an old man, a sick man, and a dead man. These experiences reveal to Gautama the suffering and limits of life. An ascetic shows him the path of spiritual quest which Gautama, after taking on the humble cloak of the monk, will follow until reaching enlightenment. **(5)** After a search of many years, Gautama attains enlightenment under a bo tree. **(6)** In the Park of the Gazelle in Sarnath, Gautama gives his first public teaching. In it, he explains the doctrine of the Four Noble Truths: Suffering, the Causes of Suffering, the Means to Overcome Suffering, and the Righteousness of These Means. **(7)** The Four Noble Truths are represented by a wheel divided into four sections.

This colossal statue shows the Buddha at the moment of his death (Parinirvana) in 483 B.C. The statue is at Polonnaruva on the island of Sri Lanka.

BUDDHA

DHARMA

SANGHA

APAN

The Spread of Buddhism

Soon after the death of Buddha, the Buddhist community divided into many schools and sects. Buddhism spread in India and was the principal religion of the country for about a thousand years. Between the fourth and the first century B.C., Buddhism reached Sri Lanka and became the main religion of the island. About the same time, the religion spread both to the southeast (in Burma and the Indochina peninsula) and to the north, reaching the Himalayan region, Tibet, China, Korea, and Japan. It also spread to the west, to present-day Afghanistan, but here the arrival of Muslims practising the religion of Islam (around A.D. 800) wiped out all traces of Buddhism.

Below: Buddhism is divided into three periods, called the three vehicles, which correspond to the three stages of the spiritual path. The Hinayana is the first period, in which are laid the basics of the religious practice. During this time, followers withdraw in order to know and improve themselves.

MAHAYANA

VAJRAYANA

The Mahayana is the second period. In this period, after having striven for improvement, the followers open themselves to others in order to help them. The Vajrayana, often kept secret, is the period in which the most difficult rituals and meditations are performed.

Left: Three important aspects of Buddhism, often called the three jewels, are: the Buddha, the principle of enlightenment; the Dharma, the path which leads to enlightenment; and the Sangha, the community of the faithful.

Finally, he saw a dead man being carried to the grave and knew the tragedy of death.

This sudden revelation of human suffering disturbed the prince. But then he saw an ascetic go by. The man was old in years but had a serene expression on his face. At that moment, Gautama Siddhartha decided to abandon the palace and his family and follow the spiritual path. He set off at once in search of an enlightenment that would free him from life's suffering. His spiritual search was long, hard, and lasted many years. Finally one day, as Gautama meditated under a bo or bodhi tree in the village of Uruvela (today called Bodh-Gaya), his mind opened, and he attained enlightenment. Others heard of Gautama's experience and began to call him Buddha, which means "the Enlightened". The Buddha spent the rest of his life preaching and trying to teach others how to overcome suffering.

The Four Noble Truths

The heart of Buddhist preaching is contained in the Buddha's first public speech. This message, which Buddha gave after attaining enlightenment, is known as the speech of the Four Noble Truths. The first of these truths is that life is suffering. The second says that the cause of suffering is mental confusion, which causes people to become attached to worldly things. The third states that suffering can be ended by removing the causes. The fourth reveals the eight-stage path by which it can be ended.

Some Jainist ascetics go naked to show their complete poverty. Members of the Svetambara sect cover their mouths with cloths to avoid swallowing insects, in order to keep their vows of non-violence toward all living things.

Mahavira, the master of Jainism

Jainism

Jainism originated through a chain of spiritual masters (Tirthamkara) that is traced back to ancient times. The main organizer of this religion was the last great master, Mahavira. Mahavira lived and preached at the same time as the Buddha. Jainism does not believe in a creator god, gives great importance to ethics, and proclaims that inner enlightenment is possible through a combination of faith in the masters, knowledge of the way the human mind works, and proper moral conduct. Jainists must respect five vows: sincerity, refraining from stealing, refraining from incorrect sexual behaviour, refraining from greed, and a non-violent way of life. Jainism never spread out of north-central India. It was formally organized in the fifth century B.C., experienced its golden age between A.D. 300 and 800, and then slowly declined. Today, the Jainist religion numbers about two million followers.

This illustration shows the burial of a nomad leader. In this scene, the burial chamber has already been prepared and its walls lined with timber.

This fragment of a felt saddle blanket is decorated with a galloping moose. (500 B.C.)

A gold ornament in the shape of a beast of prey was found west of Altai.

This wood pendant in the shape of a human head once decorated a horse harness.

PEOPLES OF THE STEPPES OF CENTRAL ASIA

Agriculture and the Shift to Nomadism

The peoples inhabiting the huge expanse of steppe covering the Asian continent north of India and northwest of China had gradually learned to domesticate animals. Still more slowly, they had learned to farm the land. About 2000 B.C., people started living in permanent settlements in houses that were partially underground. At the time, the steppe was farmed from the Ural Mountains to the Tien Shan valleys. Suddenly, around 900 B.C., the situation changed. For reasons still unknown, the steppe peoples abandoned their villages and their settled farming ways and became nomadic. They colonized the steppes with herds of grazing animals.

Economy and Art

In the west, the steppe nomads moved slowly toward the Iranian plateau. The Medes went first. They were followed by the Persians and then the Parthians. To the east, the nomads clashed with the Chinese Empire. These various nomadic peoples had similar life-styles. Many groups kept cattle, which were a symbol of wealth and social importance. Arms, harnesses, and ornaments were also similar. Meat and dairy products were staple foods, and hides were important items of trade. Raiding was also frequent.

These people owned few possessions, all of which were easily transported. However, these objects were richly decorated with plant patterns, animal representations, battle scenes, or

CASPIAN SEA

ARAL SEA

Uigarak

Ob River

Irtysh River

Lake Balkhash

TIEN SHAN

Persepolis

Ganges River

ARABIAN SEA

INDIA

• cities

⌒ burial sites

steppe region and mountain ranges in central Asia

In 1927, when archaeologists began to excavate Scythian mound-burials at Altai in Siberia, they found their contents very well preserved. Human bodies and even perishable artifacts (felt, leather, other fabrics, and wood) had been preserved by ice.

The illustrations (*left*) show why the temperature inside the mounds always remained below freezing point. Once the tomb was closed, soil was thrown over it. Next, a mound of stones more than a metre high was placed on top. Since the funerals were held in the cold season, the soil underneath the mound soon froze. During the summer, these stones allowed air circulation but kept the sun's heat from defrosting the underlying ground. During the winter, the cold stones would further lower the temperature inside the burial chamber. The ice preserved the contents.

Below: Section showing how the ground around a burial mound remains frozen in both winter and summer.

☐ mound and burial chamber
▨ frozen ground

warm air rises
descending cold air pushes warm air up and cools the tomb

Below: A mound in Pazyryk in the Altai region of Siberia.

a few human figures. The patterns were basically outlines. A few lines would define a profile or frontal image and were enough to convey the meaning of the decoration and a sense of great power.

Burial Rituals

By this time, ceremonies marking important events were very much a part of people's lives. There was often great pageantry involved. This was particularly true of the burial ritual, especially that of a leader. From the many tombs discovered, we can now picture such a funeral. First, the dead body was embalmed. In this preserved state, it was kept until the beginning of spring or autumn. Then, a rectangular pit up to 7 metres deep was dug. Inside it, a hut was built with larch logs covering its floor and ceiling. The coffin was placed inside the hut, along with rugs, pots, stringed instruments, weapons, and tables on which to offer sacrifices. After the burial, a great funeral banquet would take place.

Religion of the Nomads

The people believed the universe was watched over by the creator god Tangri. Life on earth and human destiny depended on this god, who was venerated by people throughout the Asian steppe. The universe itself was thought of as existing on three levels: the Sky, the Earth, and the Underworld. Passage from one level to the next was possible.

The person capable of passing from one level to another was the shaman. The shaman used this magical ability to intervene for the community at particularly difficult moments, such as when there was illness or when game was scarce. With rituals accompanied by drumming, imitations of animal calls, and the smoking of hemp, the shaman would descend into the Underworld or ascend into the Sky. Upon his return, the shaman would tell the people the will of the gods.

Reconstruction of a city during the Shang period. The large houses of the rulers are very different from the traditional huts of the poorer people (in the background). In the foreground is a two-horse chariot.

territory inhabited by the Shang, as shown by finds of their artifacts

Huang He

Liulige • Anyang
Erlitou • • Zhengzhou
Panlongcheng •

Yangtze River

Xi Jiang

TAIWAN

The "bi" disc was a religious symbol of the heavens (1300 B.C.).

A bronze knife inlaid with turquoise (1300 B.C.).

This small jade figurine is the oldest known representation of a government official. This figurine wears official clothing and kneels in a subservient posture.

CHINA ENTERS THE BRONZE AGE: THE SHANG DYNASTY

The First Dynasty: Myth or Reality?

About 100 B.C., the Chinese historian Sima Qian wrote the first major history of China. This history of the Chinese dynasties illustrates the evolution of the early Chinese societies. At first, during the nomadic period, people lived by herding animals. Then, a farming period began. After that came the reign of the three kings Huang, Yao, and Shun. Succeeding them was Yu the Great, who is thought to have founded the first royal Chinese dynasty, that of the Hsia (Xia), around 2200 B.C.

This first dynasty was for a long time considered by historians imaginary, a myth, like other creation myths. However, evidence of its existence has been found. In Shaanxi and in the Henan region, rough grey pottery has been found. Its complex shape suggests that it was the product of a society between the Neolithic period and the Bronze Age.

The Shang Dynasty

Around 1500 B.C., China entered the Bronze Age, with the Shang dynasty. Several elements distinguish this civilization, and knowledge of

In a foundry, workers pour melted bronze into a mould. Another worker is refining the decoration on a vessel that has been taken from its mould. In the foreground (*right*) is a large bronze vessel, cast in one piece, used to prepare food for sacrificial rituals. (Shang dynasty, 1100 B.C.)

it becomes easier because of the gradual appearance of writing. The first urban settlements rose where the various capitals of the dynasty were to develop. In one such settlement in Erlitou, the buildings represent an intermediate stage between those of the Neolithic villages and those of later imperial cities.

Today, several examples of this kind of town still exist. Each town was surrounded by dirt walls. Its buildings were on terraces and had walls made of straw mixed with mud. These imposing buildings housed government representatives. Another feature of the Shang dynasty was its preoccupation with death, funerals, and tombs. The royal tombs were especially beautiful.

During the Shang dynasty, bronze casting was developed. Many items for both daily use and for religious rituals were made of metal. They included farm tools, weapons, and vessels for cooking or for heating alcohol. The

decorative patterns were at first simple outlines like those used on Neolithic pottery. With time, the decorations became more detailed, and many showed a mythological influence. Mythological animals such as the serpent, dragon, and taotie or glutton (which devours its prey without swallowing it) as well as familiar creatures began to appear on the vessels. Similar decorations are also found on objects made of other material, such as ivory and jade. Jade, which was believed to have magical powers, was used to make the religious symbols known as bi discs.

The Shang dynasty, which included 31 rulers, eventually lost its power. With each generation, the kings became more corrupt. New clans took control, changing the name of the dynasty to avoid bad luck. The new name was Yin, which means "powerful, prosperous". This period began with King Pan Keng (around 1300 B.C.) but decline continued until the Shang (or Yin) dynasty disappeared.

Representation of the mythical "taotie" from a vessel (1300 B.C.)

Bronze Metalwork

Chinese craftworkers developed a method by which very large bronze objects could be made. Using this method, many copies of an object could also be made. In Europe, the casting mould was a single piece of clay. In China, the mould was also clay, but was made up of several sections. These sections were so precise that they fitted together perfectly. By adding or subtracting sections, moulds of different sizes could be created. Thus, there were few limitations on the size of objects that could be cast. But it was very hard to create unusual or irregular shapes with this method. This, however, was not a problem for the Chinese, who preferred intricate surface decorations rather than unusual shapes.

key territories where the Zhou were most influential during their expansion to the west

Huang He

Wei

YELLOW SEA

Yangtze

Xi Jiang

SOUTH
CHINA SEA

This map shows the sites of the fortified cities during the Zhou period. Most of the construction work took place in Zhou territories along communication routes.

THE EMPIRE MOVES WEST: THE ZHOU DYNASTY

The Realm of the Zhou

When the "warrior king" Wu took power from the last king of the Shang dynasty, he established his headquarters in the Shaanxi region further west. He proclaimed himself the protector of the civilization that was developing in the valley and along the rivers. Wu did not use violence against the conquered peoples. In fact, under the Zhou many aristocrats were able to preserve their economic, social, and even political importance under the Zhou. For this reason, the early Zhou reign seemed to continue in the tradition of the Shang dynasty, with which the Zhou had previously formed tight bonds through co-operation in war.

In order to gain power in the provinces, the Zhou did not conquer by force. Instead, they sent government representatives to these territories. Often these representatives were members of the royal family. They would settle in the new region with their families, their administrative staff, priests of their ancestral religion, and seers. Numerous cities, called "cheng cities", developed.

From excavations of the Fengchu palace in the Shaanxi region, archaeologists now have a clear picture of the administrative settlements from which the various regional capitals developed. The palace of Fengchu was composed of a network of buildings and adjoining rooms surrounded by a rectangular enclosure. It is estimated to have been built about 1000 B.C. The buildings were made of wood and cemented with a clay, stone, and straw mixture. In the centre was a large building used for ceremonies.

Bronze Objects Old and New

Besides the everyday tools and ritual vessels, a third category of bronze objects evolved. These were objects that kings or other important people had made to mark an alliance or a wedding. They were highly symbolic artifacts, inscribed with details of the celebrated event. During the Shang period, such inscriptions were limited to two or three characters. The Zhou used as many as 500 characters to describe the circumstances of the pact and the intent of those who had sealed it.

Below: A clash between a Zhou army and a group of nomads on the border. From about 800 B.C., the power of the Zhou kings was threatened by invading nomads and by the growing power of local warlords.

Left: In the court of a provincial palace, an administrator receives a concession of land. Several cities of the Zhou period have been discovered by modern archaeologists. They are similar to the one found in Qishan, which inspired this illustration.

Each territory had its own currency. The currency was made of bronze, and the most common shapes were (1) the hoe and (2) the knife. During the Zhou period, bronze objects were made not just for royal ceremonies, but for all the occasions which marked the lifetime of important people: alliances, weddings, and land deals. The quality of the bronze objects became more and more refined, as shown by, (3) a bell, (4) a ritual vase, (5) a buffalo, and (6) an elephant, all richly decorated.

For everyday use, very simple grey ceramic vessels were used. They were shaped much like those of the Shang period. But the Zhou potters did not have the skills of the earlier potters. They had lost the secret of using kaolin. Kaolin, or china clay, is a pure white clay still widely used to make fine pottery. Potters of the Shang period had mastered the art of using kaolin. With it, they made finely decorated pottery using similar patterns to those used for bronze vases.

The Eastern Zhou Period

There are still doubts among historians regarding the real power of the Zhou. Undoubtedly, their power had weakened by the time the kings moved the capital back to the Henan region in 771 B.C. They too had fallen victim to the warlike nomads from the west.

But this was not the only reason for the Zhou's loss of power. Over time, the bond between the Zhou and their administrators had weakened. The administrators became more independent, and the prestige of the king, who traditionally had been the only intermediary between the Earth and the Sky, between people and their ancestors, was now missing. Political disruption and the fall of the royal cult went hand in hand. The cities and the surrounding regions turned into small independent states. Trading and exchanges continued between the provinces, but each was now ruled independently.

CHANGES IN THE FIRST MILLENNIUM B.C.

A Period of Great Divisions

When the Zhou kings moved their capital to the Henan region, they were certainly trying to escape the invading nomads. But, perhaps without realizing it, they had also opened up the development of a new technology—that of iron. Although the Zhou dynasty continued until about 250 B.C., it gradually became less and less important. During this long period, two successive stages occurred in Chinese society. The first is the so-called Spring and Autumn period (Chunqiu, 770-485 B.C.). The second is known as the Warring States period (Zhanguo, 485-221 B.C.), and this name reflects the instability of the times.

During the Spring and Autumn period, China was divided into many small princedoms, each independent. They developed trading or hostile relationships, encouraged by the lack of any central authority. The government, in fact, was in the hands of the aristocracy (various royal clans), aloof from the farmer and servant classes.

Soon after this division, the Chinese territory began to reunite. Starting around 500 B.C., a new process of unification began. The smaller states fell into the hands of the more powerful, until, during the period of the Warring States, only seven main states survived. These were Yan, Zhao, Jin, Qin, Chu, Shu, and Qi. These states grew out of the unification of ancient and powerful smaller princedoms which were rapidly conquered or annexed. The kingdoms of Yue, Wi, and Han, for example, were conquered by Chu. The state of Lu, home of the philosopher Confucius, was annexed by the powerful Qi. Most of the wealth of the Qi state came from the forests in the mountain areas of the Shandong region and from maritime resources, mainly salt. Recent archaeological excavations of sites in small states such as Zhongshan and Zeng, which are briefly mentioned in Chinese histories, have been surprisingly productive.

Political and Economic Life

The frequency of trade, and even more importantly, the frequency of war, brought changes to the political world. These things also triggered the rise of a new social class: that of the masters. The masters were counsellors to the princes, nomadic philosophers, and dispensers of professional advice. They sold their services to those who could pay.

A new sense of relationships and alliances began to develop It was based on subtle strategic and economic balancing acts between the various princedoms. The states were constantly in conflict over border disputes.

Wealth, especially in the central states such as the Chu, was abundant. Growth in consumer goods came along with development of complex metal and lacquer techniques (metals were encrusted with all possible kinds of material). The techniques for storage of grains and fruit also improved, along with their variety. Such change took place gradually and at different rates in the different regions. Still it shows an improvement in farming methods. This was partly due to the variety of tools now used by the farmers. Some of these had been inherited from the Neolithic age but were greatly improved by the use of bronze and later of iron. The iron tools were cast, not wrought. They were cast using methods which bronze casters had been employing for about a thousand years.

The use of coins, already common in the Zhou period, increased widely in this period. Bronze, which was considered a noble metal, was often used for coins. The coins varied in size and weight from state to state, but they would often circulate between different princedoms. Like the coins of the previous period, they imitated the shapes of farming tools (the goods exchanged were mostly cereals). In some states, round bronze coins with a square hole in the centre were used. Coins of this kind were to become the official currency of the empire.

The Evolution of Chinese Society

From the Neolithic to the metal ages, Chinese society underwent major changes. The feminine element lost importance in the social environment, and the male element became predominant. At the same time, the first states, with political power over a defined territory, developed. Metal technology favoured those groups which knew how to find, transport, and melt metals. An ever-growing knowledge of metals made possible better tools, thus increasing the productivity of the land. Good tools were also indispensable for the great digging works connected with the construction of buildings and the artificial controlling of waterways.

In this way, a small number of clans and families obtained power. Walled cities developed. These were the residences of the king or of one of his representatives, who lived there with various ministers, protected by an army. The walled city in which the rulers lived separated them from the common people.

Above: Chinese metal-workers filling a mould with molten metal. *Right:* A mould for casting scythe blades.

Qin

Wei

Right below: This coloured lacquer drum and duck comes from southern China. The use of lacquer. made from a vegetable sap, spread through China in the fifth century B.C.

Yan ◆

Left: An animal ornament, made of bronze and encrusted with gold, from the tomb of King Cuo in Zhongshan (400 B.C.).

ZHONGSHAN

Zhao ◈

Wei ◈

● Jin

Qi ◈

Huang He

Lu ◻

Cao ●

● Han ◇

Left: A large bronze basin, set on wheels, from the Wu princedom (600 to 500 B.C.).

Song ◻

Zeng ●

Hiu ● Zhen ●

Huai He

◻ Chu

Yangtze

Wu ●

Yue ●

Wars between the Chinese states were frequent. Chariots and infantry fought in battles, and the crossbow, made of wood and bronze, was used more than other types of bow. Crossbows came into use around the end of the Warring States period and were to become common in the Han period.

princedom capitals during the Spring and Autumn period ●

main realms during the Warring States period ◈

lesser princedoms in the Warring States period ◻

approximate extent of Chinese civilisation ◻

Below is the reconstruction of a huge mausoleum, or burial tomb, for the royal burials in the Zhongshan region (400 B.C.). This is an example of the monumental complexes which were built in this period.

This bronze emblem was a symbol of royal power in the Zhongshan region.

As trade increased, trading centres multiplied. *Left:* A typical village market where multi-coloured glass beads (inset) were highly prized.

A gold deer, made by the people of the northern steppe, neighbours of the Chinese princedoms.

TRADITIONAL CHINESE RELIGION

The Earth, the Sky, the People, and Their Ancestors

To the Chinese, the city symbolized the world ruled by the king. It also served as a symbol of the whole universe. For this reason, each season the king would move from one part of the city to another, imitating a journey through his territories. The city was also the place where the king celebrated rituals, communicating with the Sky and obtaining his power from it. The Sky, on the other hand, also needed humankind: the Earth (square) and the Sky (round) could not remain in balance without people. People were considered the axis of the universe, and the king was, by definition, the heart of humankind.

The sense of the sacred is seen even more clearly in Chinese rural cults, especially in the cult of the ancestors. The ancestors of the Chinese people were venerated, for their experience of death. Ancestors were worshipped with special ceremonies, sacrifices, and banquets in temples dedicated to them. Initially, only the ancestors of the royal family and of the most important families were worshipped.

Death and Burial

Death was considered to repeat life as it had been on earth. At the moment of death, some souls (each individual was believed to have several souls) would stay inside the body of the dead person. This allowed the body to lead another existence, similar to the one it had on earth.

Because of this belief, important people, kings in particular, were buried with great pomp, enclosed in several coffins within a sarcophagus, or stone coffin. The sarcophagus was placed inside a burial pit of compacted soil, with walls covered by wooden boards. Objects for the dead person's use were placed inside small, adjoining rooms and on benches around the sarcophagus. These were possessions that the dead had enjoyed during life, or other objects especially made for the funeral rituals.

Horrific as the custom of human sacrifice as part of the burial ritual seems to us, it was a logical part of the reincarnation belief. The king needed women, servants, and companions to attend him. Among those usually sacrificed was a man—generally accompanied by a dog—who was placed underneath the coffins in a small room. The tomb was in the middle, with steps on three sides on which soldiers, killed on the spot, stood guard. The royal coach, with sacrificed horses and chariot drivers, rested on the slanted platform used to lower the sarcophagus into the tomb. Other burial sites near by would contain other chariots and beheaded prisoners of war, as well as ministers or friends of the dead. Only very important people were buried with such ceremony. In many tombs of common people, the dead were accompanied only by some ceramics. The habit of costly sacrifices, typical of the bronze age, disappeared very rapidly. From the Warring States period (475-221 B.C.), wooden statuettes and ceramics increasingly took the place of human sacrifices.

Divination

The art of consulting the gods or the ancestors in order to know their opinion on particular issues was very important in China. This practice was called divination. The most ancient divination practices date back to the Neolithic age, but only during the Bronze Age did they become well known. The first examples of Chinese writing are associated with them (see the chart in the following chapter). Writing was used to note the questions asked of the gods or ancestors, and especially their answers.

Several kinds of divination were used, but the development of writing corresponded to the beginning of divination using animal bones. Some flat bones, such as deer or cow shoulder bones, or tortoise shells, would crack in intricate patterns when touched with a hot stick. The stick was applied to a special spot on the bone which had been lightly carved before the ceremony. The diviners then studied the network of cracks and in it found answers to the people's questions. The questions asked, together with the answers obtained, were written on the "oracle bone" at the end of the ritual.

Gods and ancestors were questioned on all major issues. Eventually, it became customary to have divinations every ten days. The bones and shells were concealed in special hidden pits inside the palaces.

Above: The royal tomb at Anyang, seen from above. Numerous retainers, including soldiers, prisoners, servants, and friends, were killed to accompany the king into the underworld. Their corpses were placed in various places and postures throughout the tomb.

Opposite page, top: This funeral scene was inspired by the paintings on the Mawangdui silk-cloth. The richly decorated sarcophagus is in the middle of the scene. In the foreground and background are several vessels, used for the ritual offerings. Also in the background are ritual bells suspended from a frame.

Right: To get an answer to his question, the diviner touched a large tortoise shell with a glowing hot stick. Such shells were obtained from animals kept especially for divination purposes and killed during a sacred ceremony. *Insert:* This is how a shell looked after the ceremony. The writing was carved into the shell by the priest, to record the questions asked and the answers received.

The Mawangdui Silk Cloth

This cloth is the earliest-known example of Chinese painting on silk. It covered the coffin of a woman who died in the second century B.C. The main subjects shown on the cloth are as follows (from bottom to top): aquatic creatures, the funeral ceremony, the celestial veil carried by sirens, the union of the Yin and Yang dragons, the dead in the underworld, the sky supported by a bat, two wise men, some dragons, the sun with a jay, a fruit tree (*to the right*), and the moon inhabited by a toad and a hare (*to the left*).

Bottom left: A detail from the Mawangdui cloth. This is how the Chinese imagined a dead woman in the underworld, accompanied by her servants. Also shown are the Yin and Yang dragons. The union of these dragons was believed to create all living beings. In the centre, a bat supports the sky.

Below: The complete Mawangdui silk cloth.

THE CLASSICAL AGE OF LITERATURE

"Classic" Chinese Thought

During the Zhou dynasty and the Warring States period, major political fragmentation occurred in China. This resulted in the creation of many different communities. In these newly formed, independent states, the Chinese culture experienced a great flowering of the human mind. It was a period of new expression. Philosophers travelled through the communities, each spreading a new school of thought. Because of their great numbers, the group was collectively known as the "Hundred

This bronze incense burner comes from the Mancheng tomb. The top part represents the mountain of the immortals, which is the Taoist paradise. There dwell wise men who were able to reach the mountain without passing through death.

Schools." From this group emerged philosophers such as Confucius, Mencius, Lao-Tsu, Hsun-Tzu, and Han-Feitze.

Until very recently, the thoughts of these philosophers were known only through what public officials wrote about them later, when historians had taken on the task of researching and organizing the written history of China. For many centuries, historical works had been collectively referred to by the term *literature*. Such works included any text of some moral, intellectual, or scientific value. A collection of writings was classified in the first Chinese

bibliographic volume contained in the *History of the Han*. The *History of the Han* was written in the first century B.C. This bibliography, which was later reorganized, was to be the reference point for all Chinese knowledge to the present time.

The Thoughts of Confucius

The structure of ancient Chinese philosophical thought was based on teachings in five books known as the *Five Classics*. Early scholars credited these works to the great philosopher Confucius (about 551-479 B.C.).

This painted tile from a tomb at Luoyang shows two scholars having a conversation (50 B.C.-A.D. 50).

These books contain the core of the knowledge of ancient China. In them is found the ideal of a social class of which Confucius and his learned followers were the representatives. This ideal was based on a rule called the Five Relationships. The rule said that the common good took precedence over the individual's good. The rule applied to all classes. According to this rule, the community was divided into four classes: enlightened people, farmers, artisans, and merchants. The learned people were models for the other classes.

In Confucianism, humanity is the highest virtue. A ruler must follow the right principles

established in ancient times. These principles were followed in the golden age, before the decline of kings and the coming of administrators devoid of virtue. Confucius and all the thinkers of his school believed in the utility of teaching and in the possibility of progress for humankind and society.

Two Branches of Confucian Thought

The philosopher Mencius (Meng tzu) (390-305 B.C.) was the first to write down Confucius's teachings. Mencius's work had an

A master teaches his pupils who sit in a typical revering posture.

important impact upon Chinese society. Especially important was his belief that human nature is basically good.

Some decades later, Xunzi (315-236 B.C.) offered a new interpretation. Xunzi believed human nature to be evil. Because of this evil nature, Xunzi felt, people will do nothing unless they are forced to. Despite this, he believed that society could be bettered but only through education and moral guidance. He emphazied the importance of these elements in maintaining social order.

From Xunzi's thoughts, the so-called Legalist doctrine was born. Legalism, which stressed the importance of authority and strict laws, was first put into practice during the Qin dynasty. The doctrine was effective in helping the Qin dynasty expand its control throughout China and create a centralized empire.

Taoism

The Taoist religion arose along with this Confucian line of thought, which focused on the human being within an organized society. Taoism encouraged people to search for a way to live according to universal laws and not just by human laws. The word *tao*, also spelt *dao*,

originally meant "road" or "way". The oldest Taoist text is the *Classic of the Way and the Virtue (Taodejing)*. It is believed to have been written by Lao-tzu. According to legend, Lao-tzu lived about 500 B.C.

The achievements of Chinese thought between the end of the Warring States period and the beginning of the Han Empire are now well known. Archaeologists have found texts from before the empire, that reveal a variety of older traditions. The excavations at Mawangdui discovered medical and astronomical manuscripts. The excavations at Linyi have revealed works on military strategy.

Above and below: Examples of early characters found on Neolithic ceramics of the Yangshao culture.

Chinese Writing

Chinese writing bears no relationship to the spoken language. The earliest inscriptions, whose interpretation is uncertain, appear on Neolithic ceramics. Perhaps they were a kind of coded writing. Chinese writing was invented and developed during the Bronze Age as a means for preserving the questions and answers from divination rituals. Early examples are

An oracle bone, with an example of early Chinese writing.

found on divination bones.

During the Zhou period, writing became more refined, orderly, and widespread. The beautiful carved or cast inscriptions on bronze vases are the main evidence of this evolution. The ancient inscriptions were written in the small "seal" style. This means that they were still similar to the writing on seals and personal

stamps. As a result there were different forms of scripts, or writings, varying widely from region to region.

With the foundation of the empire in 221 B.C., a new script was developed from the ancient form. The unified administrative writing, or *lishu*, became the writing of the Han emperors, and between A.D. 400 and 600 it

Some writing was engraved into metal tablets.

evolved into a style now considered to be the model for elegant Chinese writing. It is still the favourite script used today, with more than 5,000 characters. Among the early writing materials were bamboo rolls. They were made of narrow bamboo strips, tied together by strings.

Early texts were written on narrow bamboo strips.

Documents written in *lishu*, a more refined form of writing developed around 200 B.C.

Maurya Empire (322-200 B.C.)

Alexander the Great's route of conquest in Asia (327-325 B.C.)

The battles fought by Chandragupta allowed him to lay the foundations of the great Maurya Empire. To the east, he fought against the Nanda peoples of the Magadha region. To the west, he battled the Seleucids, the successors of Alexander the Great.

The jewellery of this period was extremely ornate and was worn by both men and women. The gold chain with precious stones (top) has two lateral pendants. These symbols of the triple Buddhist Jewel have religious meaning, like the Christian crucifix. The necklace at the bottom is made of pearls. The three amulets in the middle are for protection against evil spirits.

Above: A village during the Maurya Empire. The people were prosperous, thanks to the vastness of the empire, which stretched from the Indus to the Ganges. Trading relationships with neighbouring countries to the east and to the west added to the wealth. The main cultivated crops were rice, wheat, millet, and sugar cane. In the background is a stupa, one of the most impressive architectural achievements of ancient India. Stupas were mound-shaped monuments. The dome was built with unfired bricks and covered with fired bricks. Stupas contained relics of the Buddha or were built over sacred places, where the Buddha was believed to have visited. The most ancient stupas date from the third century B.C.

THE MAURYA EMPIRE

India Enters History

With the foundation of the Maurya Empire in the third century B.C., it can be said that India enters history. Knowledge of its historical and human events no longer comes through mysterious legendary tales. From now on, we have precise documentation from archaeological finds, decoded inscriptions, and journals written by foreign travellers.

Chandragupta, the Founder

Between 500-400 B.C., the entire region around the Indus River came to be considered a separate province of the Persian Empire and was given the name of India. Around 330 B.C.

when Alexander the Great defeated the Persian armies, the Indian territories became part of the dominion of this Macedonian leader. Alexander and his Greek army reached the regions which today form Pakistan and the northwestern part of India.

When Alexander turned around and headed west again, Chandragupta (who belonged to an ancient clan known since Buddha's time by the name of Maurya) took advantage of this momentary confusion and put himself at the head of a liberation movement. He fought and conquered the Greek garrisons which ruled over the former Persian provinces. After freeing the western territories from foreign

rule, Chandragupta turned to the east and waged war against the Indian Nada dynasty, which ruled over the Magadha region. Then the Maurya leader stormed Pataliputra, the realm's capital (in 313 or 322 B.C.). By doing so, he founded the Maurya Empire, proclaiming himself its emperor.

Soon almost all of western India (except for the Himalaya regions and the southernmost areas) was part of Chandragupta's empire. His conquests may be considered the first true attempt at uniting the Indian subcontinent. Chandragupta organized his empire around a firm central government. The administrative structure he created operated almost un-

This sculpture is from a column of the Stupa of Sanchi.

Drawings showing the plan and elevation of the Stupa of Sanchi, one of the famous stupas of the Maurya Empire. The central part of the building was built in the third century B.C. by Emperor Asoka.

changed in all of the succeeding Indian empires. Chandragupta died in 297 B.C. One of his many children, Bindusara, was his successor. Bindusara carried on his father's politics and advanced to the south to expand the territories of the empire.

The *Arthashastra* and Social Divisions

The main source of information on the Maurya Empire is the *Arthashastra*. This text on the art of good government was written by Chandragupta's famous minister, Kautilya. The text has been preserved unaltered, and describes the political and social organization of ancient India. The *Arthashastra* speaks of a "constitutional" monarchy in which the king was the supreme head of government, with military, legislative, and judicial power.

The organization of the state was in the hands of a Council of Ministers. The council was supported by both assemblies: the "City Council" and the "Kingdom Council". The king had to consult both assemblies before he could place his seal on laws or proposals.

Culture, Religion, and Art

The Maurya Empire marks one of the most prestigious peaks of Indian cultural life. Some of the major literary works of India were written between 400 and 100 B.C. During this period, the most ancient parts of the epic poems *Ramayana* and *Mahabharata* were composed, and Patanjali wrote his basic text on yoga, the *Yoga Sutra*, and important texts on grammar. Also, textbooks on law and social behaviour, defining the rights and duties of the various castes were drawn up. The most widely practised religion was Brahmanism in all its different forms, but Jainism and Buddhism also had followers. Because wood was the chief building material, monuments and buildings did not endure the passing of the centuries, and very little Maurya art has survived. The only artistic treasures which have been preserved are the mural paintings of Ajanta in central India, and some stupas or funerary mounds.

ASOKA AND THE SPREAD OF BUDDHISM

Asoka: The Height of the Maurya Empire

The Maurya Empire reached its height under Asoka, the son of Bindusara and grandson of Chandragupta. Asoka took the throne in about 272 B.C. While still a boy, Asoka was elected viceroy for the regions of Ujjain and Taxila. By the time he became emperor, he already had some experience of ruling. Asoka, who was known to be fierce and violent, followed his grandfather's policy of expansion.

An important event in Asoka's life was the Kalinga rebellion. Kalinga was the capital of an important realm on the eastern coast of India, south of what is now Bengal. Asoka's fight against the Kalinga army was unbelievably cruel, even for those times. The realm of Kalinga suffered over 100,000 casualties, both soldiers and civilians. In addition, more than 200,000 men and women were deported. But this tremendous slaughter later filled the emperor with remorse, and he converted from Hinduism to Buddhism.

The Conversion to Buddhism

According to Buddhist sources, Asoka was converted by the monk Upagupta. Buddhism completely changed this monarch's cruel nature. Inspired and guided by the principles of the Buddha, Asoka became the most open-minded, tolerant ruler in Indian history. His reign is still remembered today as an example of mutual respect among the various religious and social factions existing in India at the time. Asoka tirelessly spread the Buddhist religion, both within his empire and abroad where he sent many missionary groups. He helped monasteries, communities, and Buddhist schools, but he was also very generous toward the Hindu and Jainist religions.

Under Asoka, Buddhism reached a summit of popularity in India. Practically all classes of Indian people were drawn toward Buddhism which for a few centuries became the most widespread religion in the empire. Asoka, although respectful of other religions, made Buddhism the state religion and favoured its spread throughout the empire's territories.

Cultural Achievements

Under Asoka, Indian art and culture of all types developed as never before. The emperor also greatly improved the social conditions of his people. He built hospitals, created irrigation systems for villages and fields, and established centres for the production of herbal medicines. He also ordered the building of the underground temples of Barabar and later donated them to the Hindu hermits of the Shiva school.

During the fifteenth year of his reign, Asoka enlarged the stupa which was raised near Kapilavastu and built many new ones. Asoka is credited with the creation of Indian writing cut into material such as metal or stone. His public proclamations were often carved on tall stone columns, many of which are still intact today. These columns were erected throughout the territories of the empire. Most of these inscriptions contained proclamations akin to moral propaganda. Through them, scholars have been able to retrace most of the history of the Maurya Empire, including important dates and events.

The Empire Under Asoka's Rule

Asoka reigned over the largest empire ever known in ancient India. Pataliputra (today called Patna) was its capital. The realm's territories stretched to the west all the way to present-day Afghanistan; to the east they reached what is today Bangladesh. The entire south-central part of India was under Asoka's dominion, with the only exceptions being the southern realms of Chola, Pandya, Chera, and Satyaputra, which were independent. When Asoka died in 232 B.C., the empire was immediately divided among his numerous sons. Within a few decades, this fragmentation was to cause the end of the Maurya Empire. Brihadratha, the last Maurya monarch, was killed by one of his generals. With his death, the golden period of Indian history ended, and a long period of political division and military tension began.

Right: Examples of people's dress in Maurya times; based on sculptures from the period. **2)** A woman wears the very common cotton veil, called an uttarya, over her head. Necklaces and bracelets decorate her neck, wrists, and ankles. **1)** This subject has given money for the construction of a stupa. He wears a mauli, the typical Indian turban tied at the forehead. **3)** A warrior wears one of the early types of tunics, tailored and sewn. Over his shoulder, he carries his sheathed sword. **4)** A woman of the royal court wears the antarya. This white cotton or linen cloth was worn by both men and women. It was held around the hips with belts and wrapped between the legs. **5)** A noblewoman's turban decorated with a heart-shaped pin. **6)** A servant girl wearing an unusual saddle-shaped hairstyle.

A lion surmounts this pillar from Kauchambi. Pillars like this are called "Asoka's pillars" because they are inscribed with the edicts of the great emperor. Some of them may actually have been set up before his reign.

An artist's reconstruction of one of the most beautiful of Asoka's pillars, the pillar of Sarnath. It is decorated with four lions and four wheels of the law.

This reconstruction is of the walls of Pataliputra, the capital of the Maurya Empire.

Buddhist monks in ritual procession around a stupa.

The rebellion in Kalinga led to great violence and bloodshed.

A fragment of a column inscribed with some of Asoka's edicts was found in Girnar. This is the oldest Indian writing.

Mahendra, the son of Asoka, was sent by his father to Sri Lanka to spread the Buddhist faith. The picture (below) shows the emperor's son explaining Buddha's teachings to the Sinhalese King Tissa and his family. The king and all of his court were soon converted to Buddhism.

Taxila

Kapilavastu

Mathura

Indus

Ganges

Sarnath

Kauchambi

Kashi

Pataliputra

Ujjain

Sanchi

Girnar

KALINGA

SATYAPUTRA

CHOLA

CHERA

PANDYA

SRI LANKA

THE SATAVAHANA EMPIRE AND THE SOUTHERN KINGDOMS

After the fall of the Maurya Empire (185 B.C.), the states of north-central and eastern India went through a long period of political and military fragmentation. Apart from mostly small local kingdoms, the Shunga dynasty, together with the Kanva dynasty, enjoyed brief periods of dominance. (Pushyamitra, who founded the Shunga dynasty, killed Brihadratha, the last Maurya ruler.) These two dynasties, however, left no distinctive mark on Indian history. More interesting was the Satavahana dynasty which ruled over south-central India (with the exception of the southernmost states) between 50 B.C. and A.D. 250.

The first Satavahana king was Simuka. After destroying the last traces of the Shunga and Kanva governments, Simuka founded his dynasty in 30 B.C. He kept the throne for twenty-three years. Simuka was followed by his brother Krishna, who conquered more territories and reigned for eighteen years. When Krishna died, the Satavahana Empire covered almost all of south-central India, and its emperors had taken the title of "Lords of the Southern Lands".

The next king in this dynasty was Satakarni, the son or grandson (according to different sources) of Simuka. Satakarni further extended his territories through various wars. Satakarni II succeeded Satakarni and was the first in a long series of kings who would consolidate the Satavahana Empire. Among them, the only one of any importance was the seventh in the dynasty, Hala, who conquered Sri Lanka around A.D. 78.

The twenty-third Satavahana emperor was Gautamiputra Satakarni, who reigned in the first decades of the second century A.D. This ruler came into power during a period of decline in his dynasty. At the time, his realm was limited to the central region, and the situation threatened to get worse. But with a series of successful battles, Gautamiputra Satakarni again expanded his empire's territory, annexing most of today's state of Gujarat. Gautamiputra gave himself the title of "the monarch whose subjects drink from the waters of three oceans". This meant that the Satavahana territories stretched from the Arabian Sea to the Indian Ocean to the Bay of Bengal.

During the second century A.D., Gautamiputra's son, Vasishtiputra Pulumayi, succeeded him to the throne. He lost some western regions but conquered more land to the southeast. The successors of Pulumayi were Shivashri Satakarni (A.D. 159-166), Shivaskanda Satakarni (A.D. 167-174), and Yajnashri Satakarni, the last great Satavahana king (A.D. 175-203). After Yajnashri Satakarni, the empire broke into many small independent princedoms.

The Kingdoms of the Far South

The far south of India was inhabited by Tamil peoples who were unaffected by the Indo-European invasions. This region was also left untouched by the expansion of the Satavahana Empire. The southernmost territories of India were divided into the kingdoms of Chola, Pandya, and Chera. The Chola and Pandya dynasties ruled in the northern and southern regions of what is now the Indian state of Tamil-Nadu. The Chera ruled the land which today forms the state of Kerala. Not even Asoka conquered these southern realms.

Sri Lanka

Since ancient times, the history of Sri Lanka has been intimately connected to that of India. Evidence of these first relationships is the Hindu epic poem *Ramayana*, where the island of Sri Lanka is mentioned as the residence of the demon Ravana. Ravana had abducted Sita, the companion of the poem's hero, Rama.

Around 500 B.C., an army from northern India invaded Sri Lanka. It was led by a monarch called Vijaya. These Aryan invaders crossed the sea, probably taking ship at a harbour located in the region of the Gulf of Cambay. At that time, Sri Lanka was inhabited by primitive peoples, whose origin is still unknown.

The invaders brought an Indo-Aryan language to the island (the Sinhalese language), as well as the Hindu religion, and even a caste system. They mainly colonized the coast and some valleys, pushing the local tribes into remote inland regions. Hinduism and the related Brahmanic rituals soon spread throughout the island. The caste system underwent some modifications in Sri Lanka. As a result, society was more or less divided into two main classes called kulina and hina. The nobles, warriors, and landowners belonged to the first class. The second class was divided into several professional subclasses, some of which had important tasks in society. At the bottom end of the scale

were the dasa, who were the slaves. Here, as in India, the slaves were used almost exclusively for housework.

The arrival of a group of Buddhist missionaries was an important event in the history of Sri Lanka. The missionaries, sent by the Emperor Asoka and led by his son Mahendra, soon converted King Tissa and all of his court to Buddhism. In a very short time, most of the population of the island had also converted.

Sinhalese art was greatly influenced by the spread of Buddhism. In fact, the Buddhist spirit inspired most of the artistic creations in Sri Lanka. Among the most important works of art are the impressive Stupas of Anuradhapura in the northern part of the island, the Buddha of Polannarukeil (a huge statue carved into a rock wall, depicting the Buddha in the act of reaching nirvana) in the central region, and the frescoes of Sigiriya, also in the central part of the island, whose style and contents are similar to Indian paintings at Ajanta.

At the beginning of the Christian era, Dravidic peoples from southern India began to invade Sri Lanka. The new invaders settled mainly in the northern part of the island. These invasions resulted in the penetrating influence of the Tamil culture and language on the island, which still has a large Tamil ethnic minority.

ARABIAN SEA

• Ajanta

• Pratisthana

DECCAN

Nagarjunakonda •   • Amaravati

Bay of Bengal

The Satavahana Empire (200 B.C.-A.D. 250) is shown in yellow-orange on the map.

A stone bas-relief from Nagarjunakonda (modern Andhra Pradesh) dates from around A.D. 300. It shows the Buddha Sakyamuni, wearing a monk's habit, being revered before a stupa.

CHERA

CHOLA

PANDYA

SRI LANKA

The peoples of India, although not noted for boat building, nevertheless made ocean voyages. Evidence of this is the colonization of Sri Lanka by Indian settlers coming from the northern territories.

INDIAN OCEAN

Heavily-armed soldiers in military dress of the period.

A court groom, wearing the typical wrap-around costume.

A prince from central-southern India, adorned with bracelets and earrings (from the Ajanta paintings).

prince

court women

A court servant with a fan (from the Ajanta paintings).

An ascetic, or sadhu, was a holy man who had taken vows of poverty (from the reliefs of Amaravati).

This map shows the trading relationships established by the Kushan Empire (*in red*), both with the Greek-Roman world to the west and with the Chinese Empire and southeastern Asia to the east. This was one of the most intense periods of trade development in Indian history.

This statue of Buddha, from the fifth century A.D., is an example of Guptan art with Mathura influence.

This statue of King Kanishka was probably originally kept inside the family temple of the Kushan kings in Mathura. The monarch is dressed in the style of the Parthians, with a tunic, trousers, a long cloak, and lined boots. He is holding two swords. The statue's head is missing as a result of vandalism by Muslim invaders who conquered the city when they overran all the territories of central-northern India.

THE KUSHAN PERIOD

After the fall of the Maurya Empire (185 B.C.), the situation in India was rather confusing. On the Ganges plain there was a group of small but independent realms with various peoples fighting and attempting to push into the country along the northern borders. Among these peoples were the Scythians who played a significant role in Indian history. They were a group of minor Iranian tribes who had come from the north. At first they pushed into western Afghanistan, but the Parthian, Macedonian, and Indo-Hellenic armies kept them temporarily at bay. When the power of these realms decreased, the Scythians crossed the border into Afghanistan. From there, they reached the Indus valley and conquered all of the territories which today form Pakistan and

the Indian state of Punjab. In 80 B.C., they stormed Taxila, then split up into several small monarchies scattered throughout northwestern India. Scythians mingled with the local populations, embraced Indian religions, and soon were no longer a separate ethnic group.

The Arrival of the Kushans

Around 126 B.C., a population of Chinese origin called Yueh-Chi invaded the Bactria region (now within Afghanistan) and settled there. In A.D. 48 one of the tribes of the Yueh-Chi, called Kushan, occupied the Indian region of Gandhara (along the course of the Indus River, the stretch of territory between modern Peshawar and Rawalpindi), driving out the last Indo-Hellenic king, Ermeo. Under

the guidance of an energetic and enterprising monarch, Kadphises I, the Kushans conquered Taxila and most of the Kashmir valley, founding a new empire which stretched from the western borders of Afghanistan to what is now the Punjab. Kadphises II increased his realm by annexing many regions of northwestern India, including the city of Mathura.

King Kanishka

Undoubtedly, the greatest of all the Kushan kings was Kanishka. He completely conquered the Indian regions of the northwest, established his capital at Purushapura (modern Peshawar), and invaded central India. He even attacked the Chinese Empire, forcing it to surrender the provinces of Kashgar, Yarkand,

Gandhara art from the third century A.D. shows Bodhisativa Maytreya carved on dark stone.

Gandhara art from A.D. 200-300: a statue of Buddha in the lotus position.

Kushan warriors, led by their commander riding in a war chariot, attack and defeat a Parthian army. From ancient times, the Indians used specially trained war elephants to terrorize opposing troops.

A Greek artist at the Kushan court works on a statue in the presence of the king and two of his guards. Gandhara art was heavily influenced by Greek styles and techniques. This influence is proof of the cultural exchanges between India and the Western world during the first centuries A.D.

and Khotan. Thus, Kanishka ruled over an empire which stretched from south-central Asia to the Ganges plain and included the Indus valley, Afghanistan, Kashmir, and the Pamir region.

Not much is known about Kanishka's administration. But from the little information that is available, it seems likely that he ruled his empire by an efficient feudal system. Satraps, or governors, were the connecting link between the provinces and the central power, and the subjects lived in prosperity. During his reign, Kanishka converted to Buddhism. He later ordered the construction of numerous stupas and monasteries. Kanish-ka was also tolerant of other religions in his empire.

Kanishka's successor was Vanishka (A.D. 168-172), who was succeeded by Atuvishka, a king who seems to have reigned for a long time over a prosperous and peaceful empire. The last great sovereign of the dynasty was Vasudeva I. He ruled from about A.D. 218-242 and was probably Atuvishka's successor. After Vasudeva I, however, the empire experienced a rapid decline, and the entire structure collapsed within a few decades.

Kushan Art: Gandhara and Mathura

The Kushan period is characterized by intense artistic activity. Two artistic styles, or schools, arose in this period, called Gandhara and Mathura. Both took their names from the localities where they developed. Gandhara art, also called Indo-Hellenic or Greek-Buddhist, applied Greek style to Indian subjects, especially the Buddhist tradition. Gandhara works of art have a lot in common with the statues of the Greek and Roman world, and Buddhist statues from Gandhara look much like Western idealizations of the god Apollo.

Mathura art, on the other hand, is wholly Indian. Especially characteristic are the images of Buddha Sakyamuni, shown seated in the lotus meditation posture. This image of the Buddha became a model for later Indian Buddhist art.

VISHNU BRAHMA SHIVA

Above: The three main gods of the Hindu Pantheon. Brahma is the Creator; Vishnu is the Preserver; and Shiva is the Destroyer.

In a scene from the *Mahabharata*, the god Krishna rides in the chariot of the warrior Arjuna and teaches him the duties of the perfect Hindu follower.

The *Mahabharata*

The *Mahabharata* is one of the two great poems of the Indian tradition. It is a collection of narrative and educational literature, which includes myths, popular traditions, and legends about the main Hindu deities. All of this material came in time to form an epic poem which describes the extended battle between two families for control of north-central India. This region is called Bharata in epic poetry, and the title of the poem refers to this name.

The date of composition of the work and the names of its authors have not yet been determined with accuracy. However, it seems likely that a version more or less similar to the present one was written in the second century A.D. The text of the *Mahabharata* is a useful source of information on the habits and customs of ancient India.

CHANGES IN THE HINDU RELIGION

The Puranic Period

About the beginning of the second century B.C., the rapid growth of both Buddhism and Jainism in India threw the world of Vedic doctrine into crisis. Its rigid structure, centred on the Brahman (the priest), no longer met the needs of the times. As a result, new ideas began to grow inside the Brahmanic tradition.

The ancient Hindu gods started to play less important roles, and new deities took their places. Especially important was the Trimurti (trinity) of Brahma, Vishnu, and Shiva. All of these changes took place without an official break from the old religion. In fact, they seemed to come from within it. Some of the new gods, such as Shiva, were not part of the Hindu pantheon before this period. But others, such as Vishnu, had been part of the ancient group of gods but were only of secondary importance. Now the new gods gained importance through slow but constant pressure from the culture that the Aryans had seemingly conquered during their invasion of India. This culture, and its ideas and traditions eased its way back into the Indo-European world. It was as if the conquered had gained revenge on the conquerors through a cultural take-over.

The liturgy itself was influenced by the change. References to the Veda's authority (see page 20) became less frequent around the beginning of the Christian era. A new collection of texts, called *Purana*, gained importance. The word Purana means "collections of the stories of the ancient times". From the Brahmanic point of view, the Purana were an extension of the Veda. They were a simple means of spreading religious teachings to

DURGA

KALI

A night with a full moon was considered especially favourable for sacred ceremonies. This picture shows village women in procession to a Hindu temple in the forest. In front of the temple sits the Brahman, the temple's keeper, who is in charge of conducting the rituals. In the background (*right*) two priests meditate in front of their caves. Beyond the trees is a village on the riverbank.

In a scene from the *Ramayana*, Rama and Sita sit in adoration before a symbol of the union of the male and female entities.

larger numbers of people. The Purana fused Indo-European traditions with the religious cultures of pre-Aryan India. The feminine elements gained importance in the Hindu pantheon. Each male deity was given a female counterpart, and new female cults developed. Cults venerating trees and water also spread.

The Hindu Pantheon

In this new dimension of Hindu religion, the trinity of Brahma, Shiva, and Vishnu is important. God is expressed through the basic forms of the three deities: the Creator (Brahma), the Preserver (Vishnu), and the Destroyer (Shiva). Each main deity has his own family, generally including a female counterpart (*shakti*, in the Sanskrit language), a special animal considered that god's "vehicle of expression", and other minor deities.

Top right: Durga is one of the main female gods of the Hindu pantheon. She has an infinite number of arms and brandishes a symbolic object in each hand. Kali is a terrifying goddess with a dark complexion and four arms. In her hands she holds the heads of the enemies of the gods, a curved knife, a bowl of blood, and a club. Around her neck she wears a necklace of skulls, and her skirt is made of arms. Kali symbolizes dynamic power carried all the way to destruction.

The *Ramayana*

The *Ramayana* is the second great epic poem of ancient India. It is composed of seven books and narrates the adventures and the heroic deeds of Rama and of his companion, Sita. Originally, it was thought that the poet Valmiki wrote the *Ramayana*. Today, however, it seems certain that the text went through several stages of development and was subject to several additions and revisions. As with the *Mahabharata*, dating the *Ramayana* is not an easy matter. Most likely, it is older than the *Mahabharata*. According to most sources, the core of the *Ramayana* was composed from 500-300 B.C. Various additions were made between 300 B.C. and A.D. 200. The adventures narrated in the *Ramayana* are still very popular in India, and they are often the subject of religious plays.

45

THE GUPTA EMPIRE

The Gupta Emperors

The Gupta period is considered the golden age of Indian history and culture. The Gupta founded an empire which covered a great part of the Indian continent. This dynasty corresponded with great development in the arts, literature, and philosophical sciences. About A.D. 400, India went through a great period of political fragmentation. As a result, a large number of small states formed, particularly in the Ganges valley. These states were often in disagreement, and they sometimes warred with each other.

One of these kingdoms was called Maghada. It was ruled by Chandragupta, who was one of the most intelligent and politically astute rulers in India's history. In a short time, Chandragupta (who reigned from A.D. 310 to 335) conquered most of the neighbouring states and expanded his realm to include most of the territory of what is today Bihar and a large part of the lands toward the Bay of Bengal. In A.D. 320, he founded the Gupta Empire and declared the city of Pataliputra the capital. This empire would last nearly two hundred years.

His successor, Samudragupta (A.D.335-375), carried on Chandragupta's unification work. With continuous and victorious battles, he conquered over thirty-five kingdoms—from the Ganges to the Indus rivers, from the Punjab to the northern regions of Deccan. Like his father, Samudragupta was a brilliant military commander and statesman. Some scholars consider him the true founder of the Guptan Empire.

Chandragupta II (A.D.375-414) combined the victories of his predecessors and completed the unification of central-western India. This included conquering the Ujjayini, a royal family who ruled over a wide territory roughly located between the central Indian region and the Deccan plateau. The capital of this realm, Ujjain, was considered the main intellectual centre of the time. After seizing this city, Chandragupta II was so impressed with its charm that he decided to make it the capital of his empire.

Social and Economic Life

Under Kumara Gupta (414-455), the successor of Chandragupta II, the refined and elegant Gupta civilization reached its height. Indian society attained a period of prosperity, of religious and civil freedom, and of artistic, literary, and architectural flowering. Moreover, the political structure itself was sound and

effective. The throne was inherited but not necessarily by the firstborn. The council of the ministers did not have executive powers, but the monarch would listen to its advice. The division of power was well distributed at all levels. The villages, which were ruled by a chief, began again to take a major role in Indian society. The importance of the cities began to decline. Meanwhile, trade and cultural exchanges were greatly enhanced.

Near the end of Kumaragupta's reign, the Huns, a warlike people from the Asian steppes, started to create pressure along the empire's borders. Skandagupta (455-467) succeeded momentarily in keeping the Huns at bay. After his death, the empire rapidly fell apart. No longer meeting any resistance, the Huns swarmed all over, reaching the Punjab region and some areas of the Rajputana region (today's Rajasthan). It was the end of the Gupta Empire.

Art, Religion, and Philosophy

During the Gupta period, Indian art underwent an exceptional period of creativity. Some of the major artistic treasures of India belong to this period (such as the Caves of Ajanta). Art was still expressing Buddhist content, but it already reflected the revival of Hinduism as the main religion in India. Although Buddhist influence was still present in art, symptoms of its decline were already noticeable. At the same time, Hinduism was gaining strength. It began to establish itself all over the country as the "true" Indian religion.

Also during this time, philosophy achieved its highest level. The Samkya philosophy is the most profound and most modern of all Indian philosophies. It saw matter as a never-ending transformation of energy and perceived the relative nature of space. The Gupta period was also the golden age of Sanskrit literature. The great poet Kalidasa (who probably lived at the time of Chandragupta II) was often invited to the Gupta court.

This detail of a fresco comes from the first Cave of Ajanta (fifth century A.D.). This cave belongs to a complex of Buddhist temples and monasteries built in a semicircle along a rocky cliff between A.D. 200 and 700. Its magnificent frescoes and statues are among the masterpieces of Indian art.

The plum-coloured areas on the map show the Gupta Empire along the Ganges River and bordering regions. The most important centres in political, artistic, and religious life are also shown. *Right, inset:* At the head of the Gupta Empire was the king, who was advised by a council of ministers. The empire was divided into provinces ruled by governors. These governors, who usually belonged to the royal family, were appointed directly by the king. The provinces were, in turn, divided into districts. Within the districts, the vital unit of Gupta society was the village, with its own chief.

KING

MINISTERS

PROVINCES

DISTRICT
DISTRICT
DISTRICT
DISTRICT

A part-view of the exterior of the Ajanta caves.

Above: Entrance to the Hindu Temple at Deogarh, from the Gupta period (A.D. 500).

The Stupa of Sarnath is one of the most famous monuments of Gupta art. At Sarnath, where Buddha gave his first sermon, there is an important Buddhist complex with numerous stupas and monasteries.

PUNJAB

Mathura

RAJASTHAN

Chambal

Ganges

Deogarh

Sarnath

Pataliputra

BIHAR

Ujjain

Narmada

BAY OF BENGAL

Ajanta

DECCAN

ARABIAN SEA

MEDITERRANEAN SEA

PERSIA

EGYPT

ARABIA

ARABIAN SEA

INDIA

INDOCHINA

BAY OF BENGAL

INDONESIA

Greater India

During the Gupta period, India increased its commercial and cultural exchanges with foreign societies. For India, these exchanges became more important and wide ranging than they had ever been before, or ever would be again. Westwards, a busy overland commerce reached as far as Egypt, Persia, and the Mediterranean. Towards southeast Asia there was a wave of expansion that led to the creation of Indian kingdoms (with the related dispersion of Hinduism and the caste system) in Indochina and Indonesia. The arrows on the map indicate directions of cultural and commercial exchange. But with the fall of the Gupta dynasty, all of this activity ended. Few traces of the Indian presence in these far-flung regions remain.

A Tibetan nomad and his son, dressed in rough leather clothing.

Top left: The Tibetans called Guru Padmasambhava "the second Buddha" because of his great importance in the history of Tibetan Buddhism. He is the symbol of self-inspired energy, of the mystical qualities of the highest forms of Buddhism, and of the final inner liberation. Padmasambhava was mainly responsible for the spread of Buddhism in Tibet.

The geographical position of Tibet is shown (in light blue) within central Asia. Its great strategic importance, situated between China to the northeast and India to the south, is obvious.

TIBET

The First Kings

We think of Tibet as being, at least until the last decade or so, the most inaccessible Asian country. The origins of Tibet are still, to a large degree, unknown. Tibet's isolation is of course largely due to the fact that it is surrounded to the south, north, and west by some of the highest mountains in the world. It seems likely that the Tibetan people derive from several nomadic tribes originating in north-central Asia.

From this world of nomads and shepherds a sort of feudal confederation began to form toward the end of the sixth century A.D. These people settled in the area along the bank of the Brahmaputra River. Soon after, they con-quered and unified almost all of the regions of central Tibet and pushed as far south as the Indian borders. Theirs was not a rigidly centralized state. Rather, it was a loose confederation in which the local princes had most of the power. The most important king of the dynasty was Song-Tsan Gam-Po. He reigned with wisdom and justice, encouraged many artistic and cultural projects, and gave the Tibetan people a written language.

According to the custom of the time, Song-Tsan Gam-Po had two wives. One was from Nepal, and one was from China. Both were fervent Buddhists and, through their efforts, the first elements of Buddhism entered Tibet. The existing religion of this nomadic

King Song-Tsan Gam-Po with (*below*) his two wives.

King Thri-Song Deu-Tsen invited Padmasambhava and other Buddhist masters to teach their beliefs in Tibet.

Above: A typical Tibetan landscape. In the background rise the high mountains, covered with snow even in the summer. At the foot of the mountains stretches a green plateau. In the distance, to the left, a monastery can be seen. Its temple stands in the middle, surrounded by monastic dwellings. Down in the valley is a nomadic camp, around which some yaks browse. Yaks are Asian wild oxen found in the Himalayan region. In the foreground, a village perches on a rocky cliff. It is dominated by the prince's palace on the summit.

During a period of persecution against Buddhism ordered by King Lang-Sarma, the Buddhist monk Vimalamitra entered the royal courtyard in disguise and began dancing. The king, curious to see what was happening, appeared at his window. Vimalamitra then killed him with a bow and arrow that he had hidden in the wide sleeves of his costume

and livestock-herding society was called Bon. This was most likely a variation of the shamanism of Asia.

Under the leadership of Gar Tsan Dombu, a descendant of Song-Tsan Gam-Po, the Tibetan army defeated the Chinese army in battle in the seventh century A.D. For about a decade, Tibet seemed about to become a great Asian empire. But as early as the end of the seventh century A.D., Tibet's strength was decreasing. China then regained all of the territory it had lost. During the reign of Thri-Song Deu-Tsen (755-797) Tibet went through a new expansionist phase and annexed several territories to the east and others to the north, towards China.

The Arrival of Buddhism

At this time, Buddhism took a firm hold on Tibet. After reading some Buddhist texts, King Thri-Song Deu-Tsen asked several Buddhist masters from India to come to Tibet and teach their religion to the Tibetan people. Some of the most renowned representatives of the Buddhist world of the 8th century came to Tibet. Among them was Padmasambhava. He played an important role in spreading Buddhism in Tibet. Soon the new religion had spread among the aristocracy and in the court.

However, the spread of the new religion also encountered strong resistance from the followers of the Bon cult. They tried in any way they could to restrain the spread of the Buddhist teachings. The tension this created was released in crowded public debates.

The most important event in the history of Buddhism's spread into Tibet is the foundation of the great Monastery of Samye. The monastery was built in the eighth century by Padmasambhava and other Buddhist masters from India. For the occasion, the first group of Tibetan Buddhist monks was ordained, and the most important texts of the religion were translated from the Indian Pali and Sanskrit languages. Within a few centuries, Buddhism was to become the heart of Tibet and its people.

THE QIN AND HAN EMPIRES

The Qin Dynasty Unites China

The first Chinese imperial dynasty was founded in 221 B.C. by Shi Huangdi (the "First Emperor"). He expanded his dominion from the state of Qin, northwest of the Central Plain, to all of China.

According to modern historians, Shi Huangdi established China's first empire ruled by a central government. In doing so, he reorganized and used ideas taken from the ancient royal dynasties. He restored the unity of power and the religious authority of the monarch as it was during the Shang dynasty. He also proclaimed that isolation was necessary for a monarch. Through withdrawal, the emperor could be free of the distractions of minor daily events and the restlessness of the world. In this way, the emperor could "empty" his inner self, so that the forces of the universe could freely act through him.

The Legalist Doctrine

During the first empire, the doctrine of Legalism triumphed. Legalism was a philosophy that emphasized authority and strict laws. These measures, which had been so effective in the Qin state, were applied throughout China. They included standardizing the writing system, currency, weights and measures, and the legal system. A network of roads connecting the provinces with the capital Xianyang (near Xian, in the Shaanxi region) was created. All imperial orders were issued from Xianyang, and the emperor ordered that the palaces of the ancient princedoms, now subject to him, be rebuilt in the capital.

The structure of the government was based on a powerful army and an emphasis on development and commercial exchange. All attempts at opposition were harshly crushed. In 213 B.C., the first minister Li Si had all of the ancient texts burned (except for essays on martial arts and technical books). He also ordered that all scholars who were "using the knowledge of the past to resist the present" should be killed. This policy of control went hand in hand with a policy of conquest. The armies of Shi Huangdi pushed their way to the borders of what is now modern China.

The Han Dynasty

The Qin dynasty survived only a few years after Shi Huangdi's death. In 206 B.C., power passed into the hands of a new family, called Han. This family ruled over China until A.D.

Above: The Great Wall was built at the end of the third century B.C. Shi Huangdi joined together existing defensive walls, which had been built by the local lords at the time of the Warring States. The Great Wall, built along China's northwestern border, formed an unbroken barrier against the invasions of the nomads. *Insert, middle:* This wall-painting shows a clash between the Chinese and nomadic armies, and a hunting scene (*lower part*). *Opposite page:* Though the army now used cavalry, the main military strength of the empire was the infantry. This army of clay warriors was discovered in 1974 inside the burial tomb of Emperor Qin Shi Huangdi in Lintong, in the Shaanxi region.

220, but its reign was divided into two periods; that of the Former Han (206 B.C.-A.D. 8) and that of the Later Han (A.D. 25-220). During the middle period (A.D. 9-25), Wang Mang seized the throne and founded the Xin dynasty.

The development of the Han dynasty was somewhat similar to that of the Shang-Zhou dynasties. The emperors established their capital first in Changan to the west (in the Xian region), and then in Luoyang in the heart of the central plain (in the Henan region). The Han continued the politics of Shi Huangdi in its basic concepts, but they ruled with the scholars, and not against them. They also continued the expansionist policy. Kings or warlords who recognized the authority of the emperor were given a gold seal as a symbol of their local power.

Much more difficult were the relationships with the nomadic tribes of the Xiongnu. These tribes were constantly raiding the northwestern borders of China, and forced the empire to

completely revise its defence system. The Great Wall had already been built by Shi Huangdi. His workers built the wall by joining fortresses built during the Zhou dynasty.

Inside the country, the Han dynasty alternately promoted the Legalist and Confucian ideas. These two schools of thought arose as a result of the chaos of the Warring States period, but they were often in conflict. For example, Legalists supported the state monopolies on staple items such as salt, iron, alcohol, and tea. The followers of Confucius preferred a more flexible economic system.

In this period, a permanent trading route connected the Mediterranean region to China. This route soon became a major channel for the exchange of people, goods, and ideas. Later on, this route was to be called "the Silk Road".

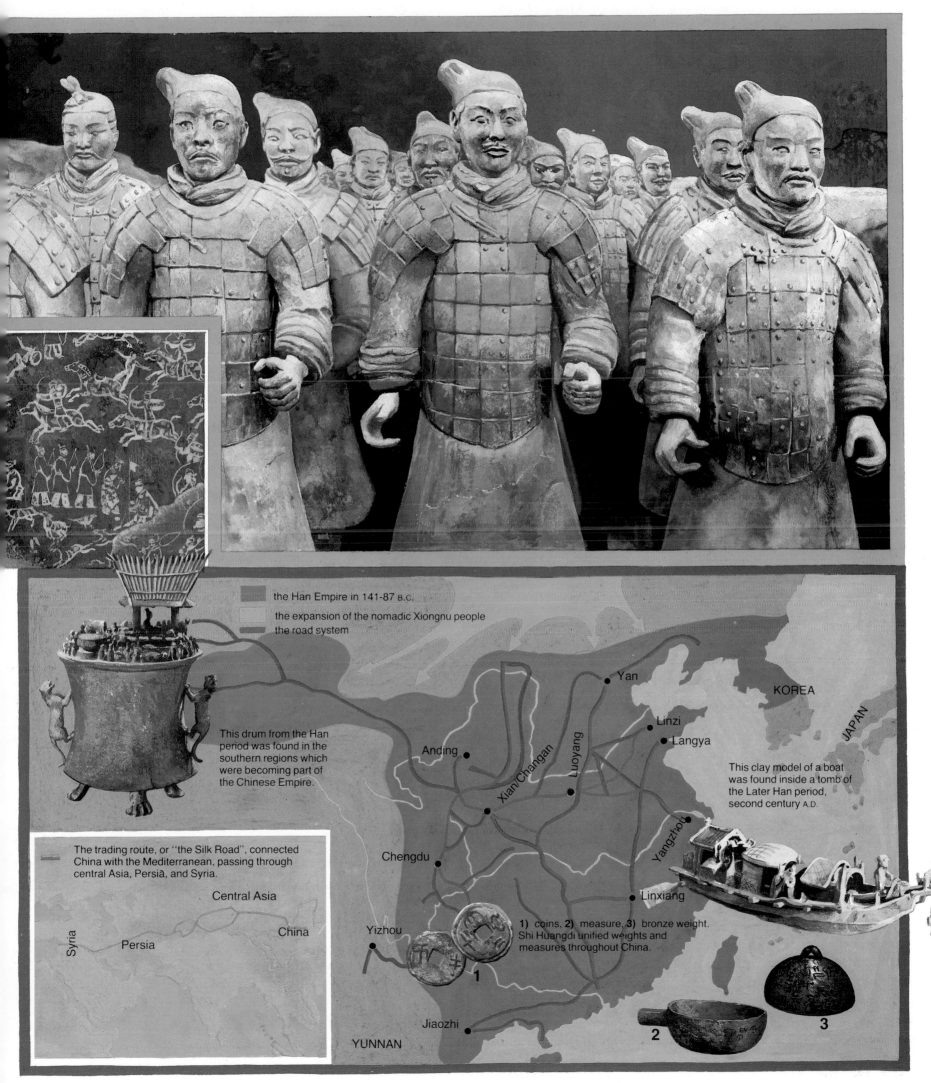

the Han Empire in 141-87 B.C.

the expansion of the nomadic Xiongnu people

the road system

This drum from the Han period was found in the southern regions which were becoming part of the Chinese Empire.

The trading route, or "the Silk Road", connected China with the Mediterranean, passing through central Asia, Persia, and Syria.

Central Asia

Syria

Persia

China

This clay model of a boat was found inside a tomb of the Later Han period, second century A.D.

1) coins, 2) measure, 3) bronze weight. Shi Huangdi unified weights and measures throughout China.

Yan

KOREA

Linzi

Langya

JAPAN

Anding

Xian/Changan

Luoyang

Yangzhou

Chengdu

Linxiang

Yizhou

Jiaozhi

YUNNAN

1

2

3

SOCIETY IN CHINA DURING THE HAN DYNASTY

The Dynastic Histories

During the Han epoch, Chinese scholars made a great inventory of knowledge. Sima Qian (145-90 B.C.) drew up the first Dynastic History, and the structure he devised was to remain practically unchanged in all of the following twenty-one histories of China, from its beginning to the modern republic.

The University

The creation of the Imperial University in 124 B.C. was in line with the thinking of the time. The University was meant to preserve the intellectual history of the nation. But it was

This jade object dates from the Han period. It represents the bi disc, a symbol of heaven.

also meant to produce, after a period of studies, good servants for the state. Students were chosen not only according to their intellectual skills, but also on the basis of some "new categories" of qualities or faults which were credited to them by a jury of wise men.

"Proper" Living

During the Han dynasty, rules were set concerning the proper use of luxury items. Material possessions were the means through which each individual was given a rightful place in the society. This rule applied to everyone, from the imperial princes (who had survived the advent of the Han dynasty and lost all powers on their lands in the first century B.C.) down to the members of the government, including the state ministers and the "kings" (rulers of the great central plain, whose authority was confirmed by the emperor but who were subject to him). The

administrators of the provinces, local officials and their deputies all had to live according to their degree of rank. The *History of the Later Han* (Hou Hansu) gives a firsthand account on the "proper" use of clothes and vehicles in imperial China. Vehicles, in particular, were an important symbol of a person's prestige.

Jade Suits and Burials

Funerals were another area where ritual was applied with extreme strictness. Burials were often planned by a person in his or her lifetime. They also exactly reflected one's social condition. The tombs of the Han nobles,

The Central Administration of the Han Dynasty

THE EMPEROR

THE THREE DUKES
High Counsellor
High Constable
High Officer of Censorship

THE MINISTERS
High Rector; rituals and astrology
High Master of Ceremonies:
subjugated princes and barbarians
Court Constable: justice
High Director of Agriculture: public finances
High Treasurer:
private finance of the Imperial family
Constable of the Guard
Commanding the personal guard of the emperor
High Coachman
Director of the Imperial Clan

of which several well-preserved examples exist, reached heights of splendour. The most beautiful are those of the Imperial Prince Liu Sheng and his wife Touwan in Mancheng (in the Hebei region), both buried in jade suits.

Each corpse was dressed in a suit made of over two thousand jade tiles fastened together with gold thread. This kind of shroud was used only during the Former Han Period (206 B.C.-A.D. 8). It was supposed to prevent the decomposition of the body according to a belief going back to the Neolithic age. The *Dynastic Histories* mention these shrouds more than once, and archaeologists have discovered more than twenty of them. They were always used for bodies of people related to the imperial family. But even here, a hierarchy was clearly defined. The threads holding the jade tiles together could be made of bronze, silver, or gold, thus revealing the social status of the deceased.

This drawing recreates the pavilion of an aristocratic residence of the Han period. Inside can be seen, from bottom to top: the servants at work; men at a meeting; women in conversation.

Below: During the Han epoch, lacquered wood was used even for tableware. This very elegant set was found in a tomb at Mawangdui which dates from 160 B.C.

Village life. In the foreground, a weaver works a pedal-driven loom, typical of those used for weaving cloth at this time.

Below: Plan of the tomb of Prince Liu Sheng (154-113 B.C.) discovered at Mancheng in 1968. The main areas are: **1)** access corridor, **2)** antechamber, **3)** carriage house and stable, **4)** central chamber, **5)** mortuary chamber, and **6)** bathhouse.

The funeral vestments of the Princess Touwan, wife of Liu Sheng, were made of jade tiles held together with a network of gold thread.

53

Nomads invade a Chinese town. Such events were frequent in the northern territories, which were threatened by peoples from the steppes moving towards the plains of the Huang He.

The Yangtze River flows through a southern landscape. In this period, the southern territories gave shelter to refugees from the north and regained the importance which they had lost at the time of the Han Empire.

THE THREE KINGDOMS AND THE SIX DYNASTIES

The Fall of the Han Empire

After its brilliant beginning as the glory of the ancient world, the Han Empire fell into chaos in the third century A.D. In particular, it suffered from economic collapse. Neither Confucians nor Legalists knew how to handle the economy which wavered between a liberal "laisser-faire" approach and government control. The economy was further weakened by long cycles of severe weather.

There was also military upheaval, as invading nomads pressed upon the frontiers. For nearly half a century (from A.D.220-265), the Chinese territory was partitioned among the "Three Kingdoms" (Wei, Shu, and Wu). During this time, the rule of the "Six Dynasties" (A.D. 222-589) began in the south. For a short time, China's unity was restored under the rule of the Western Jin Dynasty (A.D. 265-316), but the country had been devastated. It was not long before nomad invaders conquered northern China. In the period that

followed, the northern territory was divided into many smaller states ruled by an ever-changing succession of rulers. Meanwhile, in southern China, the Jin Dynasty remained in power. Gradually the situation stabilized; four dynasties succeeded each other in the southern territories, while the north was first ruled by the Northern Wei (A.D.386-534), then by the Western Wei (A.D. 534-550).

Intellectual Crisis and the Spread of Modern Buddhism

On top of the division of the country came a deep intellectual crisis. Traditional Chinese thought no longer seemed capable of explaining life, so threatened in those dark times. What solution was offered to the dreaded problem of death? Chinese thinkers, the Taoists in particular, had devised complicated theories to explain the survival of the spirit, and imagined lands of delight—true paradises only available to those who had saved them-

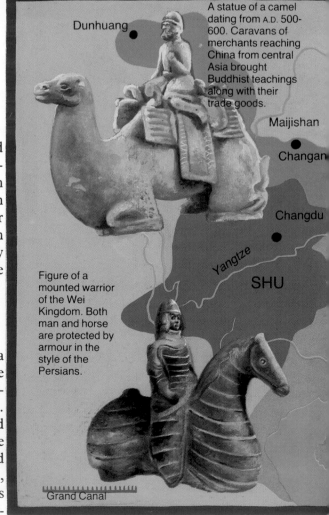

A statue of a camel dating from A.D. 500-600. Caravans of merchants reaching China from central Asia brought Buddhist teachings along with their trade goods.

Dunhuang

Maijishan

Changan

Changdu

Yangtze

SHU

Figure of a mounted warrior of the Wei Kingdom. Both man and horse are protected by armour in the style of the Persians.

Grand Canal

This clay statue of a bodhisattva is in the Grottoes of Maijishan. Maijishan, the second great Buddhist Chinese sanctuary, was built in the sixth century A.D.

The rock-sanctuary of Yungang, with its giant Buddha, was built by monks between A.D. 460 and 495.

In China, the building containing relics of the Buddha is called a pagoda. This is the pagoda of the Temple of the White Horse in Luoyang. It was the first Buddhist temple to be built in China.

The Grand Canal was an important waterway which connected Hangzhou to Luoyang and then continued northward. Its construction was started in this period.

In the third century A.D., China was divided into three kingdoms. Later, in the time of the Six Dynasties, political division further increased.

selves. But what about the common people? At this point, a new teaching brought by travellers and foreign merchants spread into China. It was Buddhism, a religion that taught control of passions.

Before true Chinese Buddhism could develop, however, it was necessary to translate the basic texts of this doctrine. When this was done, Chinese thinkers became acquainted with completely new concepts, such as that of "nothingness". The adaptation to this different way of thinking took place within small intellectual circles. In southern China, such intellectual circles were especially active, and a spiritual way of life of pure Chinese tradition was flourishing.

At this point, China was divided into two spiritual zones with differences that were stressed by the traditional Chinese scholars. Northern China was more rational, believing in the Confucian virtues of teaching and in the efforts necessary for gradual "discovery" of truth. Southern China was more mystical and Taoist-oriented and believed that enlightenment could be attained only in an instantaneous and global way. This geographical and philosophical split was triggered by the arrival of Buddhism. It was soon felt as a fact of life throughout the nation and was applied to all fields of knowledge.

The Buddhist Rock-Sanctuaries

During this period, Buddhist sanctuaries rose all over the country. The most extraordinary were the rock-sanctuaries. These small sanctuaries or cells were hollowed out of cliffs, around a huge image of the Buddha. Sanctuaries were soon in place along all of the trading routes which connected the Far East with the Mediterranean, on both sides of the Pamir mountains.

The most ancient rock-sanctuaries in China are those at Dunhuan (dating back to the end of the fourth century), Maijishan, Yungang, and Longmen. The last two contain the best examples of religious Chinese sculpture. The style of Chinese sculpture was at first influenced by Indian originals, but later tended to become more stylized.

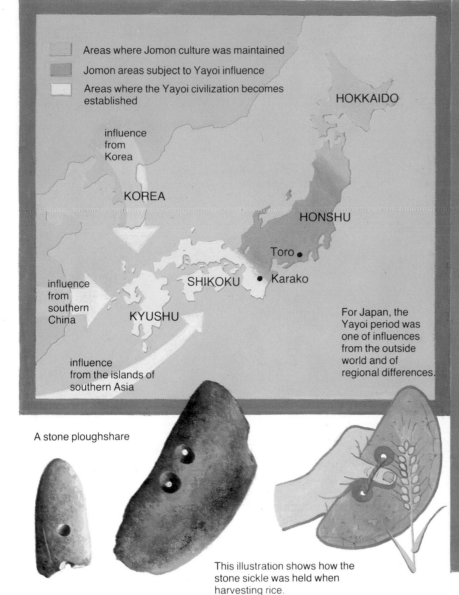

Areas where Jomon culture was maintained

Jomon areas subject to Yayoi influence

Areas where the Yayoi civilization becomes established

influence from Korea

KOREA

HOKKAIDO

HONSHU

Toro

Karako

SHIKOKU

influence from southern China

KYUSHU

influence from the islands of southern Asia

For Japan, the Yayoi period was one of influences from the outside world and of regional differences.

A stone ploughshare

This illustration shows how the stone sickle was held when harvesting rice.

A typical Japanese village of the Yayoi period

1

2

YAYOI JAPAN:
AGRICULTURE AND BRONZE-WORKING

The Late Jomon Period and the Start of Agriculture

During the middle Jomon Period (roughly 1500-1000 B.C.) many technological changes occurred in Japan. People who shaped stone, bone, and wood skilfully perfected their hunting and fishing tools. They invented an improved harpoon for catching large fish. They also improved the system of weights and buoys that had been used on fishing nets for five hundred years. Potters also showed great creativity. They created ceramics which had new shapes and patterns. Their work was an imitation, or a distant echo, of the metal vessels being created by Chinese workers in bronze during the same period.

In the middle Jomon period, a primitive form of agriculture developed on land cleared of forest by fire. Only in the late Jomon period (around 1000-500 B.C.) did rice cultivation begin. Many ceramic remains of the late Jomon period contain remains of rice grains, particularly the ones from the northern region of the island of Kyushu. Rice cultivation on flooded fields had been introduced from the middle and lower reaches of the Yangtze River (China), where rice fields had existed since 5000 B.C. Only around 300 B.C. did rice cultivation begin on a large scale in Japan, corresponding with the spread of a metal-using culture.

Within a few years, agriculture fully developed in Japan. At the same time, the potter's wheel had come into use, and metal-bearing ores were being extracted and processed. These improvements marked the beginning of a new culture in Japan. This culture, called Yayoi, started in Kyushu. The name *Yayoi* refers to the part of Tokyo in which pottery from this time was first discovered.

In the Yayoi period, corpses were buried inside large jars surmounted by a dolmen.

Left: Bronze ritual objects belonging to a chief: **1)** mirror **2)** necklace with magatama, stones in the shape of a tiger's claws **3)** two large-bladed halberd heads **4)** clapperless bell.

Above left: Use of the potter's wheel, to make jars such as this one, changed the appearance of Japanese ceramics.

Above right: A vase, decorated with human features, rather unusual for its time.

The new culture eventually spread east until it reached Honshu, the largest of the Japanese islands. But the movement was very slow and left whole areas untouched. In the regions of the northeast, the people continued a Jomon lifestyle for many more centuries. These people only began to conform to the culture of central Japan in the ninth century A.D.

The Rice Economy

Rice-growing was one of the most important advances of the Yayoi period. Rice-growing led to a settled way of life and required a stronger sense of community than did other cultures. For this reason, it seems that each village was ruled by a chief, very often a shaman woman. In the villages of Karako (in the Nara Prefecture) and Toro (in the Shizuoka Prefecture), rice is still grown today very much as it was in the past.

At this time, religion and cult practices were probably more important than war. Weapons were made, but a large quantity of the bronze artifacts from this period are not very functional. Items such as mirrors, halberds, spatula-shaped spears, and clapperless bells were probably used for rituals rather than for practical purposes.

The variety of religious beliefs is evident in the many types of burials. Some people were buried inside large single- or double-walled ceramic jars, while others were buried in stone coffins. By the end of the period, the burial sites were marked by dolmens. A dolmen is a large, flat stone, placed on similar upright stones: and similar monuments were used in Korea during this period. At the end of the Bronze Age, Korean culture was a marked influence on Japan.

THE EPOCH OF THE ANCIENT TOMBS

The First Written Information on Japan

Mention of Japan appears for the first time in the *Dynastic Histories of China* in the third century A.D. It was spoken of in the report of a journey undertaken around A.D. 240 by the ambassadors of the Chinese court of Wei, the dynasty which reigned over northern China (during the epoch of the Three Kingdoms). The travellers had explored the seas east of China and reported on the lands and the peoples they had met. They called the Japanese *woren*, meaning "dwarfs". They described in great detail the country's natural wealth and the civilization which flourished

of this. Many of these tombs are still part of the Japanese landscape today. Covered with round, square, or "keyhole" mounds, they protected the bodies of the warlords.

Each body was placed in a sarcophagus or stone coffin, dressed in full armour. Full armour included a breastplate made of iron and leather that protected the body from neck to waist, a helmet, gold and jade jewels, a quiver, arrows, and swords. Sometimes the swords had inscriptions on them. These inscriptions are Japan's most ancient examples of writing. Besides iron weapons, these warriors owned horses. The warriors' horses were as richly adorned as the warriors themselves.

from the eighth century on, these military rulers were very enterprising. In A.D. 369, they sailed to the Korean peninsula and founded a small Japanese colony, called Mimana, which lasted for about two centuries. Today, Korean scholars dispute the existence of this ancient Japanese colony.

The Emperor and the Court of Yamato

The new authority of the warlord eclipsed that of the shaman. From these innovations, the concept of the emperor was born in Japan. The emperor was the symbol of the country and was above all earthly matters. He survived

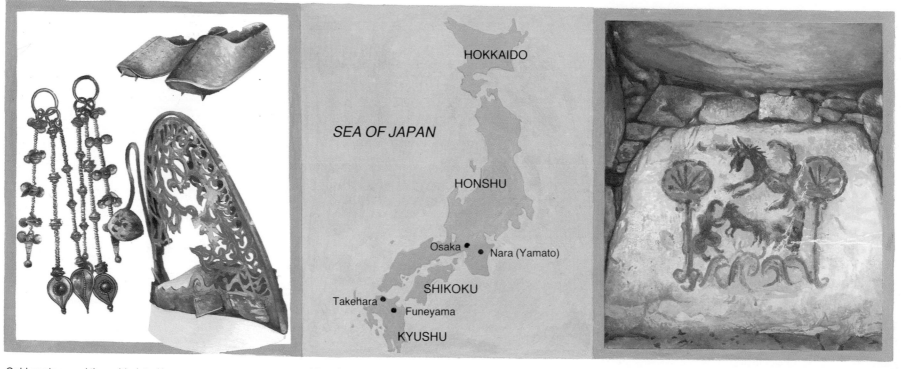

Gold earrings and the gold-plated bronze headdress and footwear of a prince were found in Funeyama (Kumamoto Prefecture).

Map showing where the objects described on these two pages were found.

A mural from the tomb of Takehara (prefecture of Fukuoka) depicts a man, two horses, and palms.
Opposite page: The great royal tombs, shaped like keyholes, of Osaka.

around the end of the Bronze Age. We learn from this account of great Japanese towns and cemeteries, and of village leaders, who were often women.

The Introduction of Iron and Tomb Burials

Between the third and fourth centuries, the Japanese began to work iron, making tools and weapons. The changes caused by this development were profound. With it came a new concept of power. The great burial mounds of the emperors Ijin and Nintoku (fifth century) and the impressive remains of ancient Japan found around modern Osaka are evidence

The tombs, like the great Chinese tombs, were guarded by replicas of servants, animals, and various miniature objects. These clay models accompanied the dead and also had a practical purpose. They helped to stabilize the mound of dirt raised above the tomb. The walls inside the tombs, especially in the northern Kyushu region, were also richly decorated. Some had paintings of geometrical patterns, while others contain scenes whose meanings are obscure.

The discovery of iron greatly changed Japanese life. The new feeling of power it inspired gave rise to a new ruling class. According to the Japanese histories compiled

all changes and revolutions.

The historical creation of the Japanese nation has been placed in the fourth century. It is symbolized by the existence of the "Court of Yamato". This was formed in today's prefecture of Nara, on the Yamato plateau. What began as only a small clan, became in time more powerful than neighbouring clans and perhaps more receptive to new ideas and technology that were coming from mainland Asia. From this clan came the ancestors of the Japanese imperial family.

A vase, decorated in relief, and typical of Japanese ceramics of this time.

1) soldier **2)** scribe **3)** horse. Clay models of these and many other figures were placed outside of the tomb, helping to keep the loose soil of the mounds in place.

A warrior in full armour stands beside a woman in court dress.

Bottom: A metal helmet like this was found inside a tomb in Osaka.

JAPAN CHANGES

More Monumental Tombs

The Yamato plateau is considered the historical heart of ancient Japan. In the fifth century A.D. the plateau was dotted by hundreds of burial mounds. Some of these mounds were up to 300 metres long and were surrounded by one or two moats. The custom of building these mounds became an important tradition in the prominent families. It lasted for at least two more centuries. Finally, the Emperor Kotoku (who reigned from A.D. 645 to 654) issued a decree limiting such expensive burials. In spite of this, mounds were built until the eighth century, as the tombs of Takamatsuzuka show. The paintings on their walls were reproductions of paintings in Chinese tombs of the same time. The fact that burial rituals continued throughout so many centuries leads historians to think that, in spite of political and technological changes, power did not change hands. Instead, the ancient clans grew increasingly stronger.

The Introduction of Buddhism

In this period, Japan was by no means isolated. It was open to foreign influences, including those of Korea and its craftworkers who fled the disruption caused by nomadic tribes in northern China. Japan also absorbed elements of Chinese civilization at a time when that civilization was flourishing. Around the middle of the sixth century (traditionally in A.D. 538 or 552), the Buddhist religion reached Japan. With it came the Sutra, which contained Buddhist teachings, and Chinese writing which the Japanese strove to adapt to their own language.

The introduction of Buddhism was not readily accepted by all of the Japanese people. Not all of the clans were converted to the new religion. Some, such as the Mononobe and the Nakatomi, resisted actively. They called Buddhism "ill-fated foreign thought" and believed it to be unsuitable for Japan. Meanwhile, other clans, under the banner of the Soga, declared it necessary to adapt to Chinese thinking. Chinese technology was already practised by Korean craftworkers and Chinese skills were well known. To the Soga clans, these skills were proof of the value of the teachings which inspired them. This resulted in a conflict between the supporters of Japanese tradition and the supporters of openness to foreign ideas. The emperor's role was

Regent Shotoku was responsible for changing Japan between the sixth and seventh century A.D. This famous illustration shows Shotoku with two of his ministers. The different heights correspond to the differing importance of the figures.

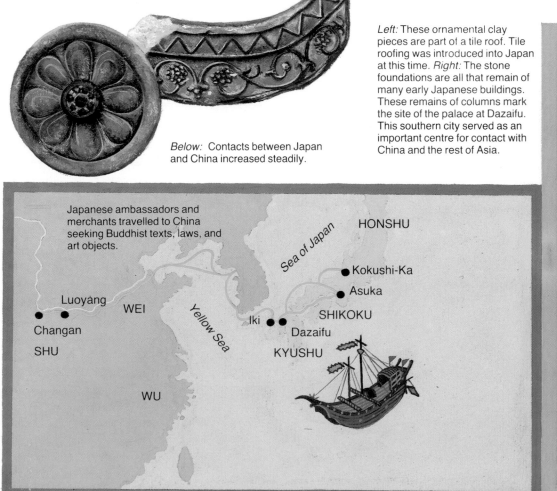

Below: Contacts between Japan and China increased steadily.

Japanese ambassadors and merchants travelled to China seeking Buddhist texts, laws, and art objects.

HONSHU

Sea of Japan

Kokushi-Ka

Asuka

Luoyang

WEI

Yellow Sea

Iki

SHIKOKU

Changan

Dazaifu

SHU

KYUSHU

WU

Left: These ornamental clay pieces are part of a tile roof. Tile roofing was introduced into Japan at this time. *Right:* The stone foundations are all that remain of many early Japanese buildings. These remains of columns mark the site of the palace at Dazaifu. This southern city served as an important centre for contact with China and the rest of Asia.

vital. He favoured the Soga's views and did not hesitate to turn down advice from the most important religious and military people in his court. It was a difficult struggle. Finally, after violent clashes and failures, the Soga clan and other supporters of Buddhism were victorious in A.D. 587.

The Regent Shotoku

A few years later, in 592, the Empress Suiko ascended the throne and reigned until 628. A tireless woman, Suiko worked toward the "modernization" of Japan. She was the first of a succession of eminent female rulers. Suiko gave herself the Chinese title of "Celestial Sovereign". She granted all powers to her nephew, the Prince Shotoku (574-622), appointing him regent.

As regent, Shotoku reorganized the government. In 603, he established twelve court ranks. The ranks, distinguished by different coloured hats, each had different functions. A year later, in 604, he gave Japan the Seventeen Article Constitution. In it, Shotoku set out ideals for government and for individual conduct. The constitution, like the twelve rank court system, clearly defined the duties and rights of the ruler, the ministers, and the people.

Regent Shotoku also tried to regulate the measurement of time, a reliable calendar being the only way history could be recorded. In the same year in which the constitution was written, history began to be computed according to Chinese custom, starting from a fixed point which the emperor would redefine from time to time. To complete his work, the Regent Shotoku opened diplomatic relations with China.

The Taika Reform

Regent Shotoku's ideas encouraged change in Japan. These changes were met with much resistance from people who feared the power of a centralized government. It was not until the Taika period (645-649) that many of these ideas became a reality. During this period, the new emperor and his supporters carried through a programme called the Taika Reform. This programme ended private land ownership. All land was turned over to the state, redivided, and parcelled out again. The new landowners were allowed to farm the land, for which they paid a set tax.

A clay pinnacle from a roof in the region of Asuka. Later, such pinnacles would be made of bronze or gold-plated bronze.

A stone sculpture of a monkey, or a god, which served as a fountain, from the Asuka region.

The custom of burying important people in large tombs continued until the middle of the eighth century A.D. *Right:* A cross section of the mound of Kansuzuka in Asuka (seventh century A.D.).

Shown here are cross sections (*top*) and the plan (*bottom*) of the mound of Temnoyama at Sakura.

Top: Izumo is one of the two oldest Shinto sanctuaries in Japan. It is on the coast of the Japan Sea, at a spot where ships from Korea and China were sure to seek harbour. The square plan of the sanctuary, with the entrance off-centre and to the right, is seen at the top right.

THE RELIGIONS OF JAPAN

The Tradition of Animism

The ancient religion of Japan was a natural cult called animism. The term *animism* was first used by British anthropologist Edward B. Tylor in his theory on the origin of religion. Animism refers to any religion in which spirits are of central importance. These spirits are often the souls of dead people. Other spirits are found in the natural world. Animism's followers often worship natural forces such as the sun, thunder, the wind, and life in all its forms, both animal and vegetable.

Shinto

The roots of Shinto, which is the oldest religion still practised in Japan, go back to the Bronze and Iron ages. The word *Shinto* literally means "the way of the kami". *Kami* has lately been translated as meaning "gods", meaning all beings who are superior to humans. Shinto followers worship many kami, who are found in natural forces. Eventually, this reverence extended to the dead, who are also considered higher beings than humans.

The Japanese gave great importance to the concept of purity, both physical and moral. Gradually, purification rituals were developed, with the objective of putting society back in order. The supreme priest of this religion was the acknowledged leader of the clans, the emperor.

Shinto ritual attained the summit of its importance with the construction of two sanctuaries, the oldest in Japan. Ise, east of the Yamato region, faced the sun and was the most

A large stone statue of two gods, a male and a female, used to cover a fountain: from the Asuka region.

Top: The Buddhist sanctuary of Horyuji at Nara. To the left is the pagoda, containing the relics of the Buddha. To the right is the kondo, the main body of the temple, where the sacred image is preserved. At the top left corner is the plan for the sanctuary, which includes the cloisters and other secondary buildings where the monks lived.

Above: This illustration summarizes the legend and reality of the foundation of a temple. Following the directions given to the emperor in a dream, the imperial messengers go to the location chosen. There, labourers and carpenters start construction. The drawing was inspired by various paintings from the fourteenth and sixteenth centuries A.D.

Left: The famous iron sword of seven points is considered the most ancient imperial symbol known in Japan. The sword is decorated with gold inscriptions in Chinese.

honoured imperial sanctuary since it housed the "Three Jewels"—the mirror, the sword, and the pearl. These were the symbols of the mystical and political power of the emperor. Izumo, which faced north towards Korea, was built on the shore of the Sea of Japan. Together the two temples reflect the concept of a dual world, male versus female, light versus darkness, as was similarly explained in China by the principle of Yin and Yang.

In Japan, the union of Shinto with the concept of the emperor began an important mythological cycle. This cycle centred around two characters: Amaterasu-o mikami, the Sun Goddess, source of all forms of life and founder of the imperial family; and Susanoo, her brother, the Lord of Darkness, the muddler and destroyer. An entire series of tales sprang up around this brother and sister, telling the story of the world's creation.

Buddhism and Its Temples

As we saw in the previous chapter, Buddhism's influence became very strong in Japan between A.D. 500 and 700. This growth was due in part to the approval granted to this religion by the emperors. In his reform plan, the Regent Shotoku attached great importance to religion as an element of unity and modernization of the country. In 594, he chose Buddhism as the national religion, following the spiritual guidance of the empress.

Shinto and Buddhism

Throughout the centuries, Shinto and Buddhism existed side by side. Shinto opposed the culture of Japan's powerful Chinese neighbours and so guaranteed a separate Japanese identity.

To preserve national unity, Buddhism had to accommodate the spiritual value of the Shinto religion. Despite the acceptance of Shinto, Buddhism remained of great importance in Japanese life and is so even today. The coexistence of these two religions is evidence of Japan's ability to create harmony from conflicting elements, one of the main characteristics of Japanese culture.

63

Shown here is a codex dating from the Taiho period in A.D. 701. A codex is an ancient manuscript of historical importance. This is the oldest Japanese codex known today. This document was important in helping scholars understand early Japanese writing.

A detail of elaborate decoration was preserved in the temple of Horyuji in the town of Nara. The painting shows symbolic events in the Buddha's life. He takes off his clothes and throws himself off a cliff. At the bottom, he offers his body to a tiger and its cubs out of compassion for the starving creatures all living beings.

THE BIRTH OF JAPANESE ART

Chinese Influence

Changes occurred in the social and religious structure of Japan between the sixth and seventh centuries. Signs of these changes were especially apparent in the arts and architecture. All over the country, Chinese culture affected local tradition. Chinese-style houses with lacquered columns and tiled roofs replaced buildings of the ancient Yayoi society. In the new religions, bronze statues replaced traditional stone statues. Even the costumes worn during official ceremonies were adapted from Chinese ceremonial clothes.

Painting

Only a few traces of the ancient paintings remain today. They are mainly decorations in old tombs, especially in the northern Kyushu region, consisting of simple shapes and symbols. But a major change occurred in 603. At that time, Regent Shotoku granted official status to Korean and Chinese artists. He entrusted them with the task of decorating the newly built temples. Thus the famous paintings of Horyuji came to be. After some decades, the Japanese artists were able to equal or out-perform their masters.

Sculpture

Buddhist sculpture, a new art, was also encouraged by the government's policy of protection and patronage. The Empress Suiko or the Regent Shotoku commissioned the first works. The statues were mainly made of bronze. Some were then gold-plated; others were left plain, under the direction of a family of artisans of Chinese-Korean origin, the Tori family.

Among the more famous works is "Triad of Sakyamuni", which was preserved in Nara. The figures in this work are frontally positioned and elongated, a typical feature of the art of the Northern Wei in China. From the Korean artists, Japanese artists also learned a different way of depicting their subjects, with more attention to smooth, rounded forms. To this, they added a distinctive grace, which can be perceived in the wooden statues—where the subjects are sculpted from a single piece of wood. Examples of this include the "Buddha of the future", preserved in the Chuguji temple of the Horyuji sanctuary, or the statues of the Koryuji temple in Kyoto.

Literature

The oldest existing written works in Japanese date from the early 700s. Prior to the arrival of the Chinese in Japan, there was no written form of Japanese. The Japanese adapted Chinese writing to create their own written language. Basically, a character in Chinese represents a whole word. The Japanese used Chinese characters to represent sounds in Japanese. Thus, a Japanese word of four syllables was written with four Chinese characters—even though those characters might have represented four separate words in Chinese. This system made Japanese writing very cumbersome, and it was difficult to learn. For a long time, only educated Japanese could read their language. As time passed, changes made to Japanese writing made it more appropriate to the spoken language.

The oldest written works in Japanese are two historical works written in 712 and 720. The first work of literature was the *Man'yoshu*, a collection of over 4,000 poems. The first fiction was written in the tenth century. Japan's greatest novel, written by a woman, dates from the early eleventh century.

The Triad of Sakyamuni is a bronze sculpture depicting the Buddha between two lesser figures. Created in A.D. 823, this sculpture is the most important image of the temple of Horyuji. It is the work of the sculptor Tori.

These three bronze, gold-plated statuettes are part of a group of forty-eight, called "The Birth of Buddha". These sculptures, created in the eighth century A.D., are also from the temple of Horyuji.

This wooden statue shows a Buddha of the future, benevolent and invincible, in the meditation position. It is believed to have been commissioned by the Regent Shotoku. It is preserved in the temple of Koryuji in Kyoto and dates from the seventh century A.D.

A wooden head of a Buddha of the future, found in the temple of Horyuji in Nara.

Detail of the head of the Buddha statue in Kyoto. The hairstyle is in the flattened, tricorn Korean style.

The main sites of Bronze Age activity are shown on this map of Southeast Asia.

In villages on the coast of southeast Asia, farming activities were complemented by fishing and trade. These activities were made possible by the construction of better boats, hollowed out from trees with the help of bronze tools.

THE LONG BRONZE AGE IN SOUTHEAST ASIA

Bronze and the Dong Civilization

At the beginning of the first millennium B.C., bronze appeared rather suddenly among the Neolithic societies of Indochina. Knowledge of the new metal came from China. People in Burma and Malaya, however, may have learned of it from India. Compared to the use of stone, the use of bronze was limited at first. But it rapidly spread.

The regions under China's influence were the starting point for the spread of bronze throughout southeast Asia. Many bronze objects were found near the village of Dong Son (Vietnam), and the name of the site is used to identify the populations which best absorbed the new technique. These people lived along the coasts of the Indochinese peninsula. The use of bronze tools improved the quality of the boats that these people used for fishing and trade. Taking advantage of the shallow waters of the internal seas and of the closeness of various islands, these peoples sailed all over the South China Sea and even reached part of the more southern seas.

Among the artifacts of this culture, bronze objects were predominant: lance heads, daggers, situlas, beautifully shaped vases. Ceramic and bone objects were also used. The detailed decorations were often of geometric patterns, but sometimes human figures were shown. The most typical objects of the Dong Son civilization were large, decorated bronze drums, which were used in rituals and religious ceremonies.

The Spread of the Dong Son People

Very little is known about the political life of this Bronze Age civilization. Only the archaeological finds indicate the extent of its spread. Certainly, the Dong Son people reached the south. They settled in Samrong Sen, Cambodia, along the Tembeling River, and reached Sumatra.

The Dong Son people are responsible for the spread of bronze in Indonesia. At first, bronze was spread only in the form of traded items. Later, the actual techniques of bronze-

Above: A bronze drum of the Dong Son culture.

working were taught to local people, inspiring the development of local metal-craft.

In the northern area of the Dong Son civilization, the ever-growing influence from China gave rise to the Vietnamese nation. The earliest Vietnamese kingdom dates back to 250 B.C. It was founded by An-Duong-Vuong, the sovereign of Au-Lac, and was very open to

This painted terra-cotta vase, of the Ban Chieng type, dates from the Bronze Age.

Above: The boat of the dead, as it appears on the bronze drum of Ngoc Lu.

A bronze lamp-holder found in a tomb at Lach-Truong near Dong Son.

The top of a bronze drum, showing the typical star pattern.

This bronze drum, which was found in Bali, is known as the "moon of Bali".

Religion and Cults

Drums and tombs tell scholars something about the important aspects of early Indochinese and Indonesian people. The drums were played during rituals before hunting expeditions or to obtain fertility of the land. For example, drums were played to ask for rain. The decorations on the drums were very important. They show shamans, the sun, water, and other symbols of rural life. The people's belief in life after death is often seen in drum decorations. The decorations show boats carrying well-dressed figures. These are the souls of the dead travelling toward the realm of the blessed, which was a great ocean to the east. The drums were also used in burial rituals, when the shaman would use his magic to descend into the realm of the dead and accompany the soul to its destination.

Tombs, another important source of information for archaeologists, were filled with many objects of daily use, so that the dead could live comfortably in the next world. The more architecturally complex tombs, built around the end of the period, were composed of three chambers. The central chamber contained the coffin. The other two contained offerings and bronze lamps with burning flames, the symbol of life.

Chinese influences. Chinese pressure gradually increased until 111 B.C. when the Han general Lou-Po-To wiped out all traces of Vietnamese authority and violently introduced Chinese culture to Vietnam. Within a few years, the Dong Son civilization disappeared completely.

The Persistence of the Stone Civilization

Although the bronze technique took hold along the coastal plains, the use of stone continued on the Indochinese plateau and as far as the island of Sumatra. In these places, its main expressions were in the form of monuments of different sizes. These monuments have been found in various sites and were often associated with burials.

The boat carrying the souls of the dead, from a cloth found at Kroe, on the island of Sumatra.

THE BIRTH OF INDOCHINA

Around the first centuries of the Christian era, the two great political and cultural centres of Asia—China and India—exerted their influence on the Indochinese peninsula. The ideas these cultures brought to the region forever changed its features. First, writing was introduced. Then the great religions of Buddhism and Hinduism spread widely, and finally, complex artistic expression developed.

The Influence of China

When China conquered Vietnam, the country was given Chinese structures, both in its political and administrative organization and in its language and writing. (Chinese became the official language, as well as the first written language of the Vietnamese.) Even economic life changed. The whole system of Vietnamese villages was modified according to Chinese models, with permanent rice fields and the regulation of water supply by irrigation.

Indian Influence

The expansion of India was prompted by trade. During the first century A.D., Indian traders discovered how to take advantage of the prevailing seasonal winds that periodically blew toward the land or towards the sea. They began to sail along Asia's southeastern coasts as far as the Sunda Islands. There they collected precious and useful goods for trade. They established trading posts where they could store their goods and replenish their food supplies. Eventually they started producing food at these sites. With the Indian people came their writing and their alphabet. Sanskrit, the Indian language, spread as a learned language and was widely spoken. The sacred texts of Hinduism and Buddhism were also widely accepted, as well as mathematical and astronomical concepts which were much more advanced than those of the local populations. Finally, even the Indian political system, built around the figure of the king, was adopted.

The States Influenced by India

During five centuries of Indian influence, numerous states came into being. They were all economically sound and lively cultural centres. The first and most important state was that of Funan. Its influence extended from today's southern Cambodia to the coast of Indonesia, to the Gulf of Siam and to southern Burma. The empire, which ended three centuries later, was ruled by Indian Brahmans and their descendants. The prevailing religion was Brahmanism, but Buddhism was also important. The Indians brought their farming and hydraulic knowledge and created rice fields and canals.

Among the other states which arose at the same time as Funan was the state of Champa. Located on the southern border of the Chinese colonies of the Tonkin region, Champa fought against these colonies in the third and fourth centuries A.D. Its land was covered by forests of spice trees, and this resource gave this state great commercial importance.

The state of Chenla, located along the middle course of the Mekong River, was originally only a small princedom within the state of Funan. At the end of the sixth century A.D., the people of Chenla, the Khmer, conquered Funan and took control of the empire. The Funan civilization, open to sea trade, was thus replaced by the closed civilization of the Khmer. Their capital was the first great architectural achievement in Cambodia, and the monuments erected there are among the oldest of Indochina.

Populating Oceania

During the first millennium A.D., the process of populating the islands of the Pacific Ocean was completed. The groups of islands scattered in the vast expanses of the ocean are usually divided into: Melanesia, comprising the westernmost islands toward New Guinea; Micronesia, including the islands north of New Guinea; and Polynesia, which includes the many islands scattered to the east.

populating Oceania

Above: A stone lintel or architectural decoration from Isanabura (seventh century A.D.).

This bronze lamp was made in Alexandria (Egypt) in the first century B.C. and found at Kanchanaburi. It is evidence of trade between the Mediterranean and the Far East.

Chinese military and political expansion from the Tonkin region south

Important sea trade routes, used by Indian merchants

Left: Head of Harihara, a god who bears the features of Shiva on his left side and those of Vishnu on his right side. This "two-faced" god is a testimony to the mingling of religions and deities which occurred in Indochina.

A stone statue of the god Vishnu found in Chiaya between the fourth and fifth century B.C. It is among the oldest Hindu images in southeast Asia.

During this time, many villages developed along the narrow coastal plains of Vietnam. Here they fell under the influence of China.

This bronze Buddha was discovered in Thailand. It shows strong Indian influence of the Gupta style and was created between A.D. 400-600.

INDIA
Ganges
Brahmaputra
Yangtze
CHINA
TAIWAN
Xi Jiang
Canton
JAPAN
Irrawaddy
Mekong
TONKIN
LUZON
PHILIPPINES
ANNAM
Isanabura
CHENLA
CHAMPA
MINDANAO
Kanchanaburi
FUNAN
GULF OF THAILAND
SOUTH CHINA SEA
SUMATRA
BORNEO
CELEBES
NEW GUINEA
SUNDA ISLANDS
TIMOR
JAVA
INDIAN OCEAN
AUSTRALIA

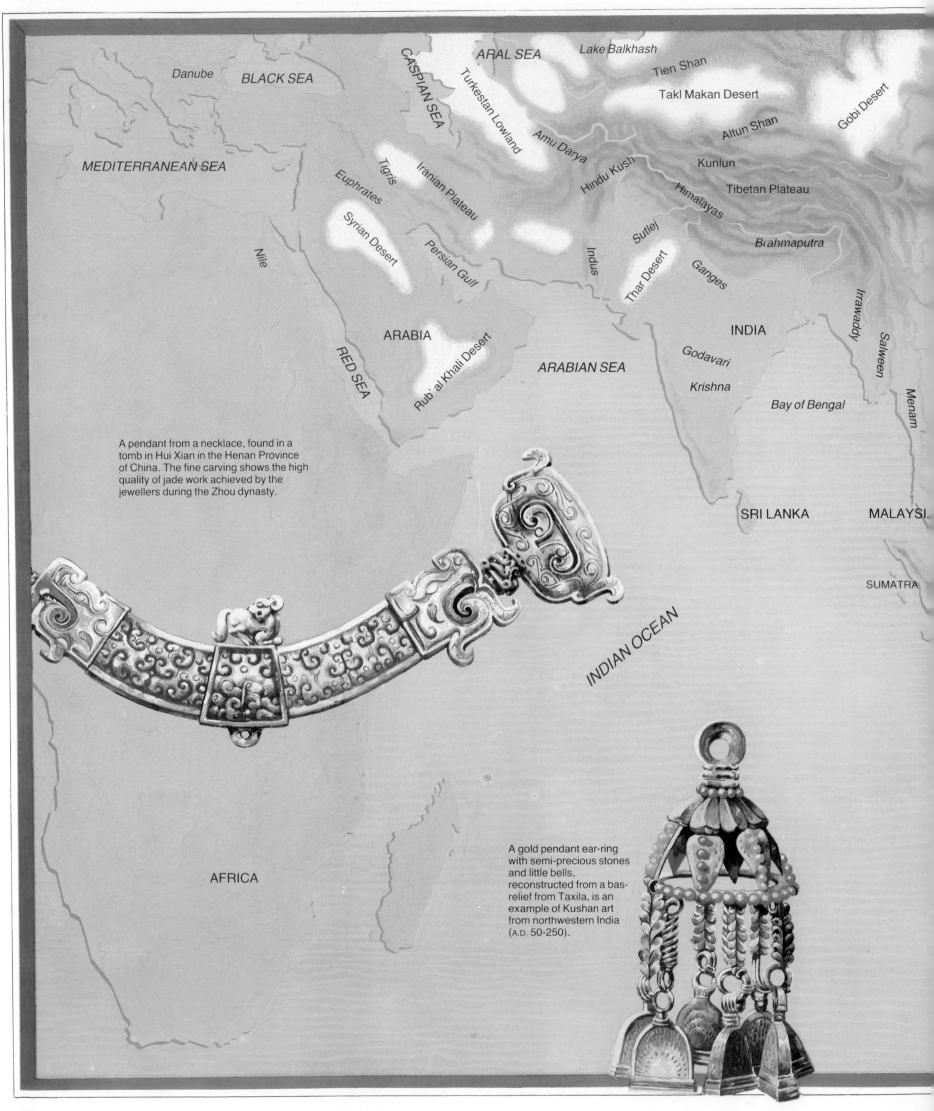

MEDITERRANEAN SEA

BLACK SEA

Danube

CASPIAN SEA

ARAL SEA

Lake Balkhash

Tien Shan

Turkestan Lowland

Takl Makan Desert

Gobi Desert

Amu Darya

Altun Shan

Iranian Plateau

Hindu Kush

Kunlun

Euphrates

Tigris

Tibetan Plateau

Himalayas

Nile

Syrian Desert

Sutlej

Brahmaputra

Persian Gulf

Indus

Thar Desert

Ganges

Irrawaddy

Salween

RED SEA

ARABIA

Rub' al Khali Desert

ARABIAN SEA

INDIA

Godavari

Krishna

Bay of Bengal

Menam

SRI LANKA

MALAYSI.

A pendant from a necklace, found in a tomb in Hui Xian in the Henan Province of China. The fine carving shows the high quality of jade work achieved by the jewellers during the Zhou dynasty.

SUMATRA

INDIAN OCEAN

AFRICA

A gold pendant ear-ring with semi-precious stones and little bells, reconstructed from a bas-relief from Taxila, is an example of Kushan art from northwestern India (A.D. 50-250).

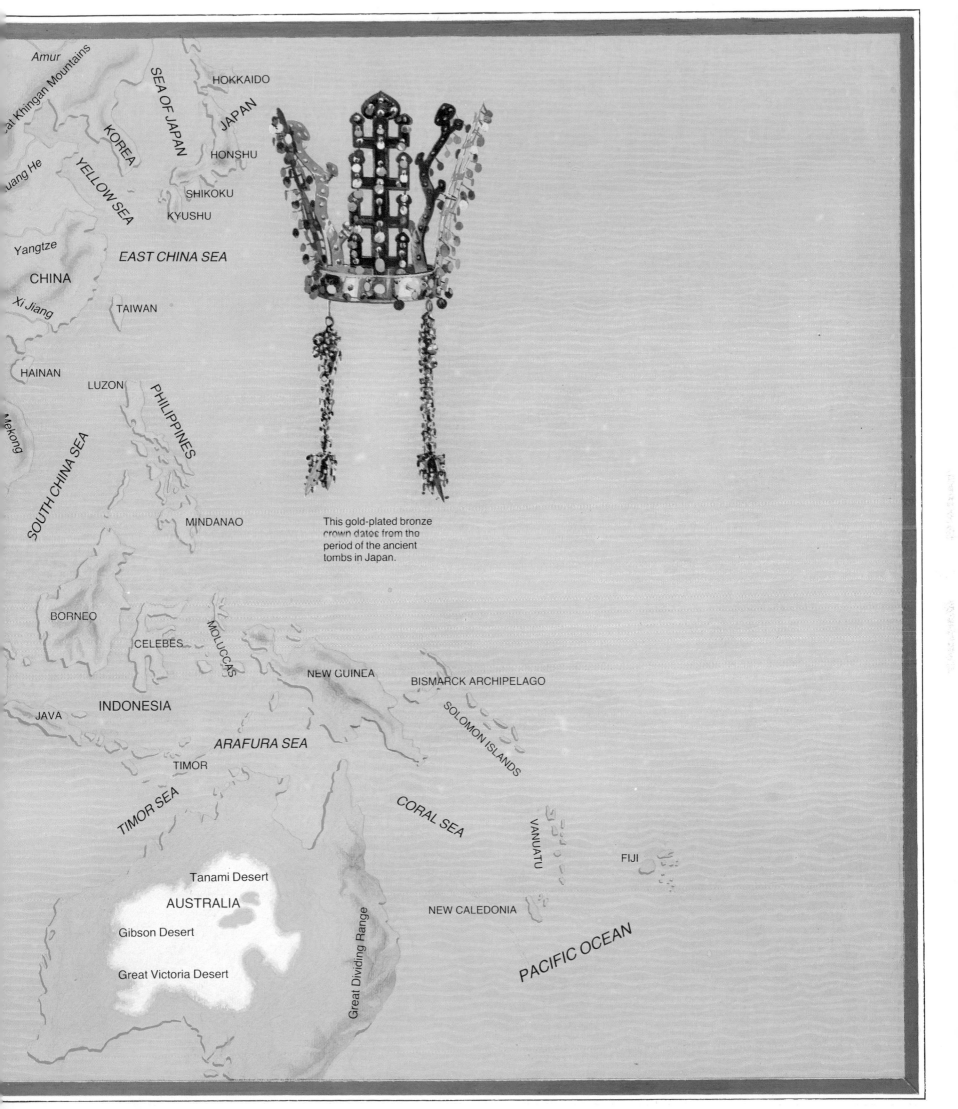

Amur

Great Khingan Mountains

Huang He

Yangtze

Xi Jiang

Mekong

SEA OF JAPAN

HOKKAIDO

JAPAN

HONSHU

SHIKOKU

KYUSHU

KOREA

YELLOW SEA

CHINA

EAST CHINA SEA

TAIWAN

HAINAN

LUZON

PHILIPPINES

SOUTH CHINA SEA

MINDANAO

This gold-plated bronze crown dates from the period of the ancient tombs in Japan.

BORNEO

CELEBES

MOLUCCAS

NEW GUINEA

BISMARCK ARCHIPELAGO

SOLOMON ISLANDS

INDONESIA

JAVA

ARAFURA SEA

TIMOR

TIMOR SEA

CORAL SEA

VANUATU

FIJI

Tanami Desert

AUSTRALIA

Gibson Desert

Great Victoria Desert

Great Dividing Range

NEW CALEDONIA

PACIFIC OCEAN

GLOSSARY

abundant: very plentiful; more than sufficient.

agriculture: the science and activities of farming; the work of cultivating the earth, producing crops, and raising animals.

archaeology: the scientific study of the life and culture of ancient peoples. Archaeology involves the excavation and uncovering of ancient cities and other sites, with all their relics and remains.

artifacts: objects made by people, especially simple or primitive tools, containers, and weapons.

ascetic: a person who leads a life of quiet study and rigid self-denial for religious purposes; a hermit or holy man.

basin: all the land that is drained by a river and its branches. Water collects near a basin to form lakes.

caste: separate social classes based on birth and wealth. The caste system was a typical feature of the Vedic culture of India.

cavalry: fighting troops mounted on horses.

ceramics: the art of making objects of baked clay, such as pottery and earthenware. Ceramics were perfected in India and Southeast Asia between 2500 and 1000 B.C.

continent: one of the principal land masses of the earth. Africa, Antarctica, Asia, Europe, North America, South America, and Australia are regarded as continents.

crossbow: an ancient weapon consisting of a bow set on a wooden stock. The stock holds an arrow and is notched to pull back the bowstring, which is released by a trigger.

cult: a systematic ritual of religious worship.

culture: the customs, art, and philosophies of a given people at a certain time in history; civilization.

currency: the medium of exchange, or money used, in any country or region.

decade: a period of ten years.

deity: the state of being a god; having a divine nature.

destiny: fate; that which will certainly happen to any person or thing.

divination: the process of attempting to foretell the future or the unknown by magical, mystical, or religious means.

domesticate: to tame wild animals and breed them for a variety of purposes. Pigs and cows are examples of domesticated animals.

dominion: rule or power to rule; supreme authority; a territory or country which is governed by a ruler.

dynasty: a series of rulers who are all from the same family; the period of time during which a specific family rules.

ecology: the relationship between organisms and their environment. The science of ecology is now recognized as an important study of the natural balance of life on earth, and how to preserve it.

environment: the circumstances or conditions of a plant or animal's surroundings. The physical and social conditions of an organism's environment influence its growth and development.

epic: a long narrative poem in a formal style about the brave actions and adventures of a traditional or historic hero or heroes.

epigraph: an inscription on a building or monument; also a motto or quotation at the beginning of a book or chapter.

epoch: the beginning of a new and important period in history; a period of time considered in terms of important events, developments, or persons.

equator: an imaginary circle around the earth, equally distant at all points from both the North Pole and the South Pole. The equator divides the earth's surface into the Northern Hemisphere and the Southern Hemisphere.

evolution: a gradual process in which something changes into a different and usually more complex or better form. Groups of organisms may change with the passage of time so that descendants differ physically from their ancestors.

excavate: to make a hole or cavity by digging; to uncover by digging or clearing away layers of soil.

fossil: a remnant or trace of an organism of a past geological age, such as a skeleton or leaf imprint, embedded in some part of the earth's crust. Scientists search for fossils as a way of learning about past life.

graphics: the art of making drawings according to mathematical rules and principles.

harpoon: a spearlike weapon used in hunting whales and large fish. The early Japanese perfected the harpoon for catching large fish.

humid: containing a large amount of water or water vapour; damp. Warm air currents floating through coastal areas produce a humid climate.

hydraulic: operated by the motion and force of a liquid.

inscription: something engraved. Many Japanese swords from the third to fourth centuries carry inscriptions.

kiln: a furnace or oven for drying or baking something, such as ceramics, bread, or bricks.

lacquer: a varnish obtained from certain trees in China and Japan used to give a hard, polished finish to wood.

lava: melted rock which flows from an erupting volcano.

legend: a story handed down for generations among a people and believed to be based on actual happenings.

loess: a very fine and fertile soil found mainly in North America, Asia, and Europe. Loess is deposited primarily by the wind.

melancholy: the condition of being sad, gloomy or depressed.

mercenary: hired soldiers; soldiers paid to fight battles in foreign countries.

migrate: to move from place to place in search of food and shelter. Migration usually revolves around seasonal changes.

minority: a small portion of an otherwise large group; less than half of the whole.

mint: to make money or other currency which is authorised by the government.

moat: a deep, broad ditch dug around a fortress or castle. A moat is often filled with water as a protection against attack.

monarch: the chief ruler of a kingdom or empire, such as a king or queen.

monologue: a long speech delivered by one person. Ancient Greek actors often delivered monologues.

monsoon: a seasonal wind of the Indian Ocean and Asia, blowing from the southwest from April to October, and from the northeast during the rest of the year.

nomad: a member of a tribe or people having no permanent home, but roaming about constantly in search of fresh grazing for animals, or food for themselves.

oligarchy: a government run by a few select people.

oracle: any person who is believed to be capable of communication with the gods.

orator: any person who is skilled at delivering speeches in public.

patrician: in the society of ancient Rome, a member of a noble or prominent family. Most political positions in Roman times were held by patricians.

peninsula: a land area almost entirely surrounded by water. Some peninsulas are connected to the mainland by a narrow strip of land called an isthmus.

pessimism: the attitude towards life that the worst will always happen; the belief that more bad than good exists in the world.

plateau: a high, level stretch of land.

plebeian: in the society of ancient Rome, one of the common people or the lower classes.

polis: a city-state in ancient Greece. Involvement in the business of the polis meant involvement in politics.

polytheism: the belief in or worship of many gods or more than one god.

prehistoric: referring to a period of time before recorded history.

primitive: of or existing in the beginning or the earliest times; ancient.

produce: fresh fruit and vegetables.

prologue: an introduction; the first part or portion of a literary work used as preparation for what follows.

retreat: to move away from a place of danger towards a place of safety.

revenue: income; the money which a business or government is able to generate for itself through taxation, profit, and other sources.

ritual: a system of acts or procedures, especially with regard to religious worship.

sanctuary: a place of peace or safety; a haven or place of rest; a special building set aside for holy worship.

Sanskrit: an ancient literary language in India dating from the fourth century B.C. Sanskrit is still used today by the followers of the Buddhist religion.

savanna: a grassy plain having only a few trees, especially in tropical or subtropical regions.

shaman: a priest or medicine man who is believed capable of communicating with good and evil spirits.

steppe: any of the great plains of Southeast Europe and Asia, having few trees.

temperate: a climate which is neither very cold nor very hot.

terrace: a flat platform cut into a hillside, used to increase the amount of farmland available in mountainous regions.

INDEX